Better Homes and Gardens.

decorating ideas under $50

Meredith. Books
Des Moines. Iowa

Decorating Ideas Under $50

Editor: Vicki Christian
Contributing Writers: Jana Finnegan, Jody Garlock, Jan Walker
Associate Design Director: Todd Hanson
Graphic Designer: David Jordan
Copy Chief: Terri Fredrickson
Publishing Operations Manager: Karen Schirm
Edit and Design Production Coordinator: Mary Lee Gavin
Editorial Assistants: Kaye Chabot, Kairee Windsor
Marketing Project Managers: Aparna Pande, Isaac Pertersen,
   Gina Rickert, Stephen Rogers, Brent Wiersma, Tyler Woods
Book Production Managers: Pam Kvitne, Marjorie J. Schenkelberg,
   Rick von Holdt, Mark Weaver
Contributing Copy Editor: Joyce Gemperlein
Proofreaders: Gerard Walen; Sarah Enticknap, Stacie McKee
Indexer: Steve McGraw

Meredith₀ Books

Executive Director, Editorial: Gergory H. Kayko
Executive Director, Design: Matt Strelecki
Senior Editor/Group Manager: Vicki L. Ingham

Publisher and Editor in Chief: James D. Blume
Editorial Diector: Linda Raglan Cunningham
Executive Director, Marketing: Jeffrey B. Myers
New Business Development: Todd M. Davis
Executive Director, Sales: Ken Zagor
Director, Operations: George A. Susral
Director, Production: Douglas M. Johnston
Business Director: Jim Leonard

Vice President and General Manager: Douglas J. Guendel

Better Homes and Gardens₀ Magazine

Editor in Chief: Karol DeWulf Nickell
Deputy Editor, Home Design: Oma Blaise Ford

Meredith Publishing Group

President: Jack Griffin
Senior Vice President: Bob Mate

Meredith Corporation

Chairman and Chief Executive Officer: William T. Kerr
President and Chief Operating Officer: Stephen M. Lacy

In Memoriam: E.T. Meredith III (1933-2003)

All of us at Meredith₀ Books are dedicated to providing you with information and ideas to enhance your home. We welcome your comments and suggestions. Write to us at: Meredith Books, Home Decorating and Design Editorial Department, 1716 Locust St., Des Moines, IA 50309-3023.

If you would like to purchase any of our home decorating and design, cooking, crafts, gardening, or home improvement books, check wherever quality books are sold. Or visit us at: bhgbooks.com. Titles you might be especially interested in are:

- Style on a Budget
- Decorating Ideas Under $100
- First Home Style
- 3-Ingredient Decorating
- Flea Market Decorating

Lucky you! Your decorating style isn't constrained by the dictates of any certain designer, your parents, your friends, or the latest trend of the moment.

You delight in expressing your own individual look—whether it's urban, shabby chic, traditional, fun and funky, or eclectic. Your only concern, like most of us, is watching your budget.

That's why you're going to LOVE this book!

Every single idea you'll discover, from living places to sunny spaces, from powered-up paint to windows with wow, is dazzling, doable—**and under $50.**

So come unleash your creativity. We've got great ideas, whether you want to do a lot or just a little. Paint your living room aubergine or use a worn workbench as a coffee table. Cover that tired old easy chair with a vibrant tablecloth. Use mismatched flea market bottles to display peach-colored roses in your entryway.

Then add those finishing touches that *make* a room—for pennies. Clip family photos to a chain and string between light fixtures. Pour shimmering sea glass into dimestore tumblers to anchor colorful candles. Wrap an old lamp with rope for texture.

It's easy. It's cheap. And it's so much fun. Because when your guests admire your decor and asked who did it, you'll say, "I did—for less than $50!"

The entryway of your home reflects you and your lifestyle. You get to decide how fun, fabulous, and fantastic to make it.

Love French-country style? Get a white distressed table and cover it with candles and family photos in hand-me-down frames. If you're into urban looks, go for sleek and shiny with chrome and glass. For a touch of cottage chic, toss colorful pillows on a loveseat. Make it elegant, vintage, or urban—but make it yours.

jazz up your entryway

Go ahead. Be creative. Use clever thrift shop and flea market finds to welcome guests with an unexpected touch of whimsy:

- **Buy a round decorator table** for about $8 at a home discount store and cover it with vintage fabrics or remnants of an old quilt you picked up in a secondhand store.
- **Grab a long, unfinished shelf** for about $12–$15 at a home store, paint it a complementary color to your welcome area, and display your prized collectibles— be they '50s-era globes, colorful country crocks, a variety of old bottles in various bright hues, or Dresden blue plates.
- **Improvise architectural elements** by getting a variety on sale at a crafts or hobby store for $5–$35, depending on size, and mount them in your entryway. Faux urns, columns, cherubs, and cornices work well.

- **Avoid painting by** shopping wallpaper stores for new fool-the-eye murals that recreate everything from beach scenes to woodland retreats. Go online and search for "murals." You'll pay $20–$50 to do an average-size entryway.

USE WHAT YOU HAVE Add nature's beauty. Top a rustic branch table with a variety of seashells you've collected on family vacations, *right*. Add fresh flowers from your garden to a container you already own for a fresh, no-cost look to welcome your guests.

thrifty entryway treatments

Consider these ideas using unexpected, yet pleasing, techniques:

- **Use a bold accent color** against a neutral palette. A secondhand chest painted Chinese red pops against off-white walls. A collection of white and red candlesticks of varying heights would tie the two together.
- **Liven up the blandness** sometimes found in newer homes with special painting techniques in brave new colors like seafoam, aubergine, or seacoast blue.
- **Colorwash, rag, or sponge** to give spectacular effects for less than $50. *(See Chapter 4 for how-to instructions on these and other special painting methods.)*

spectacular stairs

To help your stairs step up in style, consider these low-cost ideas:

- **Stencil the front of each stair** with a contrasting color of paint. You can draw your own or purchase stencils at craft and hobby stores for less than $5.
- **Turn a dull stairwell** into an irresistible passageway by painting walls a bold color. Feeling brave? Mask off contrasting stripes.
- **Use the wall above the landing** to bring the eye up the stairs by displaying a colorful poster or inexpensive framed art there.
- **For holiday magic,** entwine the railings with white netting (available at fabric stores for less than $1 a yard). Then string tiny white twinkle lights (just $4 for 100 lights at some fabric stores) over and under the netting for a holiday wonderland feeling.

PAIR UP PRINTS Handsome botanical prints are the focus in this gardener's entryway, *left.* Get three pictures of the same subject and frame them with finds from a home discount center ($6–15 a frame). Then hang them equally placed over furniture. The cowboy boots are a fun contrast to the white table and stately pictures.

FRESHEN WITH FLOWERS Take a round table ($5–$15 at home discount stores) from simple to sensational, *above,* by adding a cheerful floral tablecloth ($2–$5 at garage sales). Top it with a secondhand crock filled with colorful flowers from your garden to brighten up your entryway.

The hours you spend at home may be few, so make them count with stylish, welcoming spaces that reflect your personality. These easy, low-cost ideas enhance the beauty of everyday rooms for extraordinary family moments. If you'd like to make some changes to your living areas, we have the ideas to help you—all under $50.

how to choose deep colors

If you're thinking of using these colors, two gallons of paint costing under $50 can make an incredible difference in the look of a room. Here's how to make wise decisions:

- **Look in your own closet.** The rich colors you wear could be a start for your room's exciting new palette.
- **Go to your local paint store** and pick up color chips (they're free). Have an open mind—choose unusual colors that appeal to you, even if you've never used that shade in decorating before.
- **Next, audition it.** Take the chips into the room you're redoing to see how you like them. Take into account the furniture you're thinking of using in that room, to see if the shade blends well.
- **If your upholstery is a light solid,** choose a contrasting dark hue for the walls. Then "knit" the new palette together with throw pillows and artwork.

- **Remember, paint often looks more intense** than it seems on the paint chip when it's rolled onto all the walls. You may want to go just a shade lighter than you were originally considering.
- **Look at paint chips** in different lighting— morning, noon, evening, artificial light, and natural light. A hue may change drastically in various illumination.
- **Bear in mind that paint usually dries darker** than it looks when it's wet. You might want to paint a sample board to get a more accurate preview.
- **Be mindful that sheen changes color.** A flat, matte paint differs from the same color in a shiny, glossy finish. The shinier the color, the lighter it will look. So keep that in mind as you're choosing your paint.

TRY RICH HUES Color isn't just for contemporary spaces. Imagine these antiques, *right*, without the plum walls. The deep color here invokes the ambience of an English country house. For an average-size living room, paint costs only about $35.

1,2,3—ready to paint!

You're probably eager to get started, but do take time to prepare your walls before you start painting. Proper preparation is the key to wonderful results: a beautifully painted room.

get the walls ready

All wall surfaces need a coat of primer if they haven't been previously painted, plus a base coat to provide an even surface for the final covering paint. Keep these tips in mind:

- **Primers seal base surfaces**, reduce absorbency, and provide a uniform finish.
- **Base coats are used as a follow-up** to the primer to further prepare the surface before using the topcoat. They reduce the amount of final covering paint needed.
- **Topcoats are divided into two types** of paints. One is water-base (latex) for plaster, wallpaper, masonry, wall, and ceiling surfaces. Oil-base paints are mainly used on wood and metal.
- **On new surfaces**, use a thinned latex and water coating as a primer.
- **On previously painted** or papered surfaces, latex paint should be built up coat by coat, allowing each layer to dry thoroughly in between coats.
- **Be sure the room is well-ventilated**, to avoid breathing paint fumes.

choose the paint

Whether you opt for a happy yellow, *left*, rich hues for a European feel, or light and bright tones to showcase cottage chic style, here are some pointers:

- **Choose high-grade paints.** They're simple to apply, cover beautifully, and last longer, saving you money in the long run.
- **Shop for paint** at reputable home centers. With routine care, newly painted surfaces can last up to 10 years.
- **Decide what paint is suitable** for the surface. Water-base (latex) paints are ideal for walls and ceilings. Oil-base paints (alkyds) are best for woodwork and metal surfaces. If in doubt, ask the store consultant.

- **Buy enough paint to do the entire job.** This is especially important if you're having paint custom-mixed for a particular color, since pigments can vary from batch to batch.

select the best finish

Flat, semigloss, and high-gloss finishes are available. Each has advantages:

- **Flat paint is good on most walls** and ceilings, except those subject to frequent soiling, such as in the kitchen and bathroom. Dark, flat paint shows stains more than light, flat paint.
- **Semigloss paint has the softness** of a satiny surface, with the durability and washability needed in heavy-use areas, such as kitchens and kids' rooms.
- **High-gloss paint has the most washable** finish, and the soil comes off most easily. It also gives a luxurious lacquer look.

estimate quantities

Generally, a gallon of paint covers approximately 400 square feet. Give the paint dealer the size of your room (the total length of all walls multiplied by the room's height) and the number of openings. Also:

- **Take into account extra space** taken up by alcoves or chimneys.
- **Include windows and doors** as part of the surface unless they're very large.
- **Allow for two or three base coats** if the surface is porous or textured.
- **Use fewer coats** for nondrip paints, because they're thicker.
- **Keep in mind that semigloss latex** may need more coats than a flat latex.

CELEBRATE COLOR This entryway, *left*, once languished dressed in plain white walls. Painting the wall the same sunny yellow in the poster helps all these great pieces pop. The cost? Just about $15 for a gallon of interior paint.

HOT TIP

When painting, include the ceiling to make the room feel more complete. A dark hue overhead creates intimacy, while lighter shades feel more spacious. If you're color-shy, add some of the wall color to a gallon of white ceiling paint; the ceiling will seem less stark and remain understated.

low-cost slipcover decorating

Are you living with outdated or damaged upholstery? Then it's time for a little undercover work. Use classy cover-ups on sofas, chairs, and ottomans to unify disparate pieces, conceal ugly fabric, or change the look of a room. (Cleaning is easy—slip off soiled slipcovers and toss in the wash.)

If you sew, search bargain bins, flea markets, garage sales, and thrift stores for affordable fabrics and make your own slipcovers. Non-sewers can check online sources, catalogs, and discount stores for affordable, ready-made slipcovers.

sew slipcovers

If you like the elegant look of the slipcovers *upper left,* and can sew, here are directions:

Materials:
Tape measure
Sheer drapery fabric (see instructions for yardage calculations)
Thread to match fabric
Sewing machine
$\frac{5}{8}$-inch fusible bonding tape
$\frac{1}{4}$-inch-wide organza ribbon

Instructions:
1. **Calculate yardage.** For seat covers, measure the seat's width and length and add $\frac{1}{2}$-inch all around for seam allowances. Draw a paper pattern to these dimensions.

2. **Multiply** by how many chairs you'll cover. Most upholstery fabrics are 54 inches wide.

3. **For the skirt side and front panel,** measure around the seat from stile to stile (chair back posts) and add 12 inches to gather the fabric at the front corners.

4. **Add twice the width** of the back chair leg and 1 inch for seam allowances. For the drop, measure the seat to the floor and add $3\frac{1}{2}$ inches. Cut the required number of panels to these measurements.

5. **Cut the skirt's back edge** to match the angle of the back chair leg. You may need to piece fabric widths to obtain the required panel length.

6. **Use the paper pattern** for the seat cover to cut the required number of covers. Finish the back edge of each with a princess seam (double-fold the raw edge as narrowly as possible and stitch). Set seat covers aside.

7. **Hem skirts.** Fold the lower 3 inches to the front (right side of the fabric) and secure the raw edge to the fabric using fusible bonding tape and organza ribbon.

8. **Starting at one short end of the skirt,** mark a $\frac{1}{2}$-inch seam allowance the width of the back chair leg, and the length of one side of the chair seat. Mark this point, then measure 6 inches and mark. Mark the measurement of the chair seat front, then measure 6 inches and mark.

9. **Using a long stitch length,** make two rows of gathering stitches in the two 6 inch areas. Pull up the bobbin threads to gather, fitting skirts to chair seats (see diagram). Stitch skirt panels to seat covers, allowing short ends to extend beyond the back edge of seats by the width of the chair leg plus the seam allowance (see diagram).

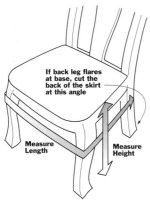

If back leg flares at base, cut the back of the skirt at this angle

Measure Length

Measure Height

Step 3

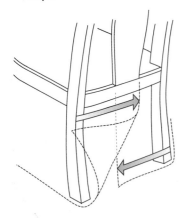

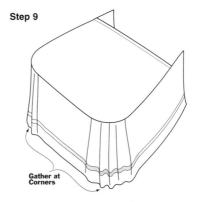

Step 9

Gather at Corners

Step 10

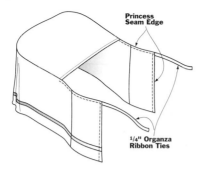

Princess
Seam Edge

¼" Organza
Ribbon Ties

10. For the skirt back panel, measure from the outside edge of each back leg to the center back. Add 3 inches for overlap plus ½-inch seam allowances on the side and top edges, and 3 inches for the hem. Cut two pieces of fabric to these measurements.

11. Fold and iron hems. Stitch back sections to front and side panels. Finish raw edges with princess seams. Stitch a 20-inch-length of organza ribbon to the top outside edge of each back skirt piece.

12. Tie skirts to chairs, wrapping the ties around the center backs of chairs.

GIVE 'EM THE SLIP The living room, *below,* takes on a cool attitude with white canvas cover-ups. For the dining chairs *on the opposite page,* sheer skirts downplay the brown wood. It takes 6 yards for the dining room slipcovers, so figure on spending $12–$47, depending on the material you choose.

low-cost ways to display your treasures

If you've ever driven for hours across a long, flat state, then you know that an empty, level horizon line gets boring fast. That same thinking translates from the road to your rooms—so use your collectibles to create exciting terrain indoors.

The trick is to incorporate elements into your decor that are a variety of heights, textures, and colors. Try to make sure attention is drawn all around the room—pieces are high and low, smooth and textured, muted and bright. Here are a few thrifty ways to show off your collectibles:

- **Walls can become canvases** or backdrops for bold displays. For instance, three cornice-style plate rails mounted on the wall can show off a plate collection. To add depth and variety, position smaller items with more vertical shapes along the edges.
- **A rusted metal stand** that once held food orders at a diner can be repainted and used to display a collection of old postcards or black-and-white family photos.
- **Glass bottles** can be randomly strung on wire to hang inside a window where they catch the sunlight. Use bottles of varying sizes and shapes. Wind wire around the neck of the bottle and secure the wire on the window frame, using nails. Put additional bottles on the windowsill.
- **Small shelves in various sizes** can hold interesting items, from bunnies and bulldogs to children's books or thimbles. Paint new ones in complementary colors, or collect worn ones with peeling paint for a vintage look. Home improvement stores offer a wide variety from $4–$17 each.
- **An old hay feeder** from a farm auction or junk shop can be mounted on the wall to hold a book collection.
- **A time-worn window** salvaged from the curbside or a thrift shop can be mounted on a wall and used to display collections of plates, records, old bowling pins, farm implements—you name it.
- **Windowsills** make a perfect, no-cost backdrop for collections of small objects, such as miniature chairs or tiny animals.

USE STACKS OF BOOKS A low plane, such as this fireplace hearth, *left*, gains interest with stacks of books to prop up items. You can also use decorative boxes to elevate your treasures—at no cost.

HOW TO
age an unfinished bench

1 Lightly sand it.
2 Distress the surface by randomly striking it with a hammer or chain.
3 Brush on a base coat of color; let dry.
4 Rub the edges (or any place natural wear occurs) with a candle.
5 Apply a topcoat of paint in a different color; let dry.
6 Gently sand off the top coat anywhere that you applied candle wax, so the base coat color shows through slightly. (The wax will make it easier to remove the paint.)

Note: Sand and paint the bench in the direction of the wood grain.

COFFEE TABLE STAND-IN An unpretentious wooden bench, *above*—whether new and unfinished or a vintage find—can stand in as a relaxed coffee table in the living room, family room, or den. You can probably find one at a flea market or the Salvation Army for less than $50.

go prepared for bargain shopping

Before you set out on your trek for thrifty treasures, consider these top tips from seasoned bargain-hunters who've gone before you:

- **Use a backpack** for your purse, car keys, bottled water, and other necessary items so your hands are free.
- **Wear old clothes**—you may bump into dusty or rusty stuff.
- **Skip the glam shoes** and wear comfy ones—your feet will thank you at the end of the day.
- **Take cash in small denominations** along with your checkbook and credit cards. Some vendors only accept cash.
- **Clear out your car** so you have room for your beautiful buys.
- **Stash bubble wrap** and old newspapers in the trunk of your car so you can wrap breakable items for a safe ride home.
- **Consider taking a small suitcase** on wheels to make toting purchases easier.
- **Be prepared** to dig through piles. Often the best items are buried under the slower-selling ones.
- **Consider shopping the entire area** if the sale is large, or has many booths, before you buy anything. You may see something at the end that's a better price, or that you like more.
- **Bring a small notepad and pen** or pencil to write down the names, prices, and locations of items you may want to revisit.
- **Take a second walk** around the show or shop about an hour before closing. Vendors may have had a slow day and be more willing to negotiate prices.

HOW TO
negotiate

If you're lucky, folks having garage sales or thrift shop owners may be willing to negotiate prices (sometimes at least 10 percent less than the original price marked). Keep these tips in mind when you're wheeling and dealing:

1. **Be polite.** Good ways to ask about a discount are: "Is the price firm on this?" or "Is this your best price?"
2. **Pull a Meryl Streep acting technique** if you spot something you really love. Don't show too much interest or comment excitedly on it, or you may cut your chances to bargain for a lower price.
3. **Don't try to bargain** if a sign says, "Prices Firm."
4. **Ponder buying more than one item** from a dealer. You might get a better price. It never hurts to ask.
5. **Never make a ridiculously low offer,** such as half. It's likely to annoy the proprietor enough not to take anything at all off the price.

try terrific trunks

You could purchase an ordinary side table for sitting beside a sofa or an easy chair, but this tactic with trunks—or vintage suitcases—is much more creative, as well as practical and affordable. Farm sales offer some of the best deals in old trunks, chests, and suitcases. Stack them up as end tables and use the interiors to store:

- Books, magazines, and scrapbooks
- Linens and sheets
- Carefully wrapped extra dishes
- Toys and out-of-season clothes

You can put these items on the tops of trunks with level surfaces:

- Lamps and family photos
- Beverages (with protective coasters)
- Collectibles

Be open to various styles of trunks. Many international and import shops offer inexpensive, unique trunks made of rattan, bamboo, or wicker.

SUPER TABLE SUBSTITUTES Use the unusual vintage suitcases, *right,* to make a terrific table. Likewise, the painted trunks, *left,* offer great storage, add character to any room, and are a great furniture bargain for $10–$50.

HOW TO
develop your style on a budget

1. **Learn about the elements of good design**—it doesn't cost a thing. Stroll through art galleries, museums, and fine furniture stores. If you can't afford the top-end items, you'll still start to be able to recognize well-designed items when you see them.

2. **Notice pieces with good proportions** and pleasing lines as you explore. You'll soon learn what's good quality and what isn't.

3. **Start a collection** of styles and ideas you like. Collect popular decorating magazines and tear out pictures that appeal to you. You'll probably discover that you gravitate to a particular style, whether it's urban, new age, or farmhouse.

4. **Less is more,** especially when it comes to furnishings. The pared-down approach is not only an elegant type of interior design, but it also costs less money because you don't need as many pieces. A limited number of furnishings also creates a sense of spaciousness and relaxation.

5. **Get one great piece** you fall in love with to start decorating a room. It could be a stained-glass window, a pedestal column, or an antique headboard—the possibilities are endless. Chances are it could be the focal point of your decor, and you can look for other furnishings that fit in well with that piece.

6. **Mix and match.** Don't think everything in a room needs to be one color or style. Vintage and modern, cottage chic and chrome—lots of times it's the jolt of unusual combinations that give your rooms their unique style. Plus, the eclectic mix-and-match look lends itself to incorporating thrifty finds from junk shops, farm auctions, and other inexpensive shopping places.

budget ideas for ottomans

You can use ottomans in various colors and designs to add continuity to your decorating, or to contrast what you have. Here are a few thrifty ideas:

- **Shop garage sales** and "scratch and dent" rooms of local furniture stores for ottomans well under $50.
- **Make a slipcover** for a secondhand ottoman out of parachute material (cheap at military surplus stores). Then get creative with colorful acrylic fabric paints from a crafts or hobby store.
- **Redo an old ottoman** you already own by re-covering it with sheets or linens.
- **Top off one you have** with a great scarf or fabric remnant.

other ottoman options

- **Line up a trio** of matching ottomans in front of the sofa and use them to prop up feet or serve as a coffee table (use a tray on top for stability).
- **Position an ottoman** on each side of the sofa or chair as side tables.
- **Use ottomans beneath a window** as an impromptu window seat. When guests come calling and you need extra seating, ottomans easily move anywhere.
- **Dark colors and patterns hide** spills and soil, and may be the best choice if you have young kids.

FLEXIBLE SEATING Any room can benefit from a few ottomans. They perform many functions without gobbling up lots of floor space. Go to local secondhand stores or the "scratch and dent" room of your local furniture store for bargains.

HOT TIP

Some ottomans contain secret storage: lift off the top cushion to reveal space for stashing books, magazines, games, a blanket, small pillows, or even your knitting.

make a handy project kit for under $50

If you're into do-it-yourself, thrifty decorating, you'll eventually want to prepare yourself with the basics you'll need for various home projects. With these, you'll have a great start. You can find them at the best prices at home discount or home improvement centers—watch for sales.

- **Can opener** to open cans of paint. Sometimes you can get one free when you buy paint, so be sure to ask. **(About $3 if you can't get it free from the store.)**
- **Caulk.** Choose a paintable acrylic or acrylics combination for indoor surfaces. It's used for sealing around bathtubs, sinks, and windows, as well as filling gaps between baseboards and walls. **(About $1.50.)**
- **Crafts knife.** These are retractable single-blade knives with replacement blades. They'll help you get a clean cut on thick materials such as mat board or foam-core board. **(About $2.)**
- **Glues.** Get a variety. For gluing fabrics, check crafts and fabric stores for washable fabric glues. For general purpose gluing of porous surfaces such as wood and paper, thick white crafts glue works well. For gluing wood to wood, use carpenter's glue. Five-minute epoxy is suggested for gluing nonporous surfaces such as metals, glass, porcelain, tile, and plastic. **(About $7 for two kinds.)**
- **Hammer.** A 16-ounce claw hammer is a good all-purpose tool. **(About $4.99.)**

- **Hot-glue gun.** Every do-it-yourselfer needs at least one. High-temperature glue produces the strongest bond and won't soften when exposed to sunlight or heat. For the greatest versatility, choose a dual-temperature gun that uses both low- and high-temperature glues. **(About $3.99.)**
- **Paintbrushes.** Choose a good-quality natural or synthetic-bristle brush for major painting projects. **(About $6.)**
- **Painter's tape.** This low-tack masking tape leaves no residue after removal. Use it to mask off areas where you don't want paint to go while you're painting adjacent areas. **(About $3 a roll.)**
- **Safety goggles.** Always wear these when scrubbing with heavy-duty cleaners, sanding wood, using furniture stripper, or painting a ceiling. **(About $5.)**
- **Screwdriver.** Look for cushioned, easy-grip handles and fracture-resistant bars and tips. **(About $2.)**

- **Pliers. (About $3.)**
- **Sewing needles and pins.** Keep a box of dressmaker's pins, sewing needles, and heavy duty large eye or tapestry needles. Quilter's pins are good for upholstery fabrics because they're extra long and have large plastic heads that are easy to see. **(About $3.)**
- **Tack cloth.** Check hardware stores for this loosely woven cloth that's been treated to be slightly sticky so it will pick up sanding dust. **(About $2.)**
- **Tape measure.** You'll need a flexible plastic or cloth tape with a metal end. **(About $3.)**

WELCOME WICKER Some wicker furniture (new and old) is still less than $50. Pieces such as this wicker chair and tables, *left,* are available at home centers, yard sales, and flea markets. See how to paint them *below.*

HOW TO
spray paint wicker

1 **Spray paint outside** or in a well-ventilated garage.
2 **Move items** (cars, tools, etc.) out of the way before you start, or cover them with a drop cloth, since you'll probably spray outside the piece you're working on.
3 **For a smooth, drip-free finish,** shake the can well and hold it above the surface at a distance of 8–12 inches.
4 **Point the nozzle** toward the surface, depress the button, and sweep the spray onto the piece, applying a very light layer to avoid drips.
5 **Move your arm smoothly** back and forth to keep the paint application evenly distributed. Stop spraying at the end of each sweep, then start again for the next sweep. This helps prevent drips and build-up along the edges.
6 **Let the piece dry** thoroughly before applying additional thin layers.

before after

ROOM RE-DO Try what these homeowners did—repurpose rooms to fit your family's real-life needs and activities.

repurpose your rooms—for free

It's not often that you find decorating ideas for free, but here you go. Keeping an open mind about each area in your home, and using it for a different activity or living space can mean more room, convenience, and usability—at no cost whatsoever.

The original layout pictured here, *left,* featured a living room, dining room, and large combination kitchen/family room. But the new owners really needed a playroom for toddlers, located so the parents could supervise them while doing other work.

As these owners thought about repurposing the area, they analyzed the layout. Here are the lessons they learned that could well apply to your home.

the specifics

- **Think location.** For example, is putting an eating nook in a crowded kitchen the best idea? Maybe it could be tucked into an adjacent family room for a less-cramped feeling. In the scenario on these pages, the former dining room is in the right spot to serve as a playroom. This way, the kids are supervised by adults in the living room.
- **Create a focal point.** Here an inexpensive colorful tent (under $50) serves the purpose perfectly. And there's plenty of space for the baby swing and a wide variety of other toys.
- **Consider the traffic flow** in and out of the room. Here the owners put up baby gates to control traffic. A gate on the living room side protects good furniture and keeps art objects off-limits.

baby-proof decorating*

Babies learn quickly. Turn your back for a moment, and the infant squirming helplessly on a blanket is crawling across the room at high speed. Look at your surroundings from a youngster's point of view. Then baby- and child-proof your home with this advice.

- **Check that crib bars** are no more than 2⅜ inches apart to prevent infants from getting their heads stuck between them. Cribs manufactured after 1974 must meet this and other safety standards.
- **Ensure that the crib mattress fits tightly,** with no gaps for an infant to fall into. Keep the crib clear of plastic sheets, pillows, and large toys—they can be suffocation hazards.
- **Place an infant's bed away from windows.** Check for potentially hazardous pull cords and install devices if needed.
- **Use child safety gates** at the top and bottom of all staircases and be sure they're installed correctly. Avoid accordion-style gates with large openings that children could fit their heads through.
- **Keep surfaces free of small objects** that could be swallowed. Such objects include coins, button-size batteries, rings, nails, tacks, and broken or deflated balloons.
- **Keep electrical cords and wires out of the way** so toddlers can't pull, trip, or chew on them. Cover wall outlets with safety caps.

*From the National Safety Council. For more information, visit them online at **nsc.org.**

HOT TIP

Hang colorful note cards on a plastic chain to decorate the walls in children's rooms. As your kids begin drawing, add some of their artwork— they'll be proud you're displaying their creations.

IRVING PENN

THE SHAKER WORLD: ART, LIFE, BELIEF ABRAMS

PERIOD ROOMS IN THE METROPOLITAN MUSEUM OF ART

HELEN LEVITT · MEXICO CITY

ELEMENTS
OF STYLE

a passion for pattern   Kristin Cargill

low-cost storage solutions

These days, it seems everyone has one basic decorating problem in common: Way too much stuff, and nowhere to store it. Here are some ideas you might want to use:

- **Under the bed.** Lidded woven baskets make excellent under-the-bed storage, as do thrifty plastic, lidded containers.
- **Beneath stairways.** This space is great for items not often used, such as holiday decorations, seasonal clothes, or extra sets of dishes and linens.
- **The back of doors.** Today decorative hooks come in a wide variety of styles and finishes, from contemporary steel to country French. You'll be surprised how many jackets or pajamas you can fit on the back of the door with design-wise hooks.
- **Over-the-door organizers** are handy for shoes in a bedroom, toys in a child's room, pantry items in the kitchen, and gift wrap supplies in a crafts room.
- **Metal or plastic shelving.** For long wear and service, look for well-made, smooth, plastic-coated metal shelving or heavy-duty plastic shelving. Colors typically are white, tan, or other neutrals.
- **Roll-out shelving.** Available at home discount centers, it comes in a range of widths and tiers, and works well for bringing items in the back to the front.

COZY CORNER SPACE Organize a work corner with this thrifty desk, *left.* The wooden sawhorses are about $10 each, and you can find pre-cut glass at hobby or crafts stores for about $25. See directions *below.*

RECYCLE AN ARMOIRE Consider recycling an old armoire or cupboard you already own, like the one *far left.* The shelves can hold work supplies or clothing. If you keep the door open, decorate the inside like a wall space. The good news? It's free.

HOW TO
make a sawhorse desk

With the addition of a glass top, sawhorses can become a clean, modern desk.

1. **Buy two wooden sawhorses** from a home center and paint them white.
2. **Set the sawhorses** in place.
3. **Measure for the size** of the top. You'll want the glass to extend beyond the sawhorses several inches on each side.
4. **Find pre-cut glass** in an oblong shape at hobby or craft stores.
5. **Place the glass** over the sawhorses.
6. **Optional:** Place clear plastic "bumpers," available at hardware stores for several dollars, between the sawhorse tops and the glass to keep the glass from slipping and scratching.

nifty alternatives to a new sofa

When you think about living room furniture, don't automatically think "new sofa" as your only seating space. The average new lower-end sofa costs $400—$600.

You can do better—with a little patience and creativity. Here are some ideas to get you started—you'll save at least $400 over buying a new couch!

1 **USED SOFAS.** There are lots of good used ones out there. Maybe the owner moved, and the sofa style or color doesn't fit the new decor. Or perhaps there's just no longer room for it.

By shopping local thrift shops and garage sales, you'll find great possibilities for $30–$50. If the fabric is worn or you don't like the color, you can always cover it with your own used sheets and tablecloths, or find usable fabrics at secondhand stores.

2 **WORN CHURCH PEWS.** Sometimes you can find beautiful wooden ones at auctions, starting at about $40. You might want to call older churches in your area to see if they have any for sale. Or visit **www.usedpews.org** on the Web, where some are available for $50.

A USED GLIDER OR WOODEN GARDEN BENCH can star in the family room or den for casual seating. You can spray-paint the wood in vibrant colors to go with your decor. Get some fabulous fabric at a secondhand store and re-cover pillows you already own for easy seating. You can find vintage benches and gliders online at ebay.com for $17.99–$40.

TWO COMFY USED CHAIRS. You should be able to pick these up at thrift shops or garage sales for $15–$25 each, and cover them, if needed, with bedspreads or sheets you already have.

TWO DELUXE COTTON CAMP CHAIRS (new) for about $15 each, in coordinating colors. If you're into wide-open spaces, this could easily blend with a nature-themed decor. Spray-paint a wide resin patio table, about $12, a related color and presto—you have a cute seating area that brings the feel of the outdoors inside your living space.

HOW TO
create $ensible chic

1 **Mix formal pieces with more primitive ones** for stylish comfort. For example, a worn carpenter's bench with clean lines can be used in front of a classic sofa, if colors tie the pieces together.
2 **Don't necessarily pitch things with missing pieces.** Pots, sugar bowls, and tureens without lids make wonderful vases with character.
3 **Decorate with outdoor furniture** for less money and more pizzazz. Try a couple of vintage metal lawn chairs ($8-$20 each) in a sunroom for extra seating. Or get a plastic lawn table (less than $10) and spray-paint it a bold, primary color for a kid's room nightstand.
4 **Add bargain Eurostyle.** Secondhand finds such as a damaged 18th-century clock face can be hung on a wall as an architectural element.
5 **Use unusual items** to add splashes of color. For instance, used sap cans in bright colors can be used on a living room wall to create a real-object painting. You can find them online at ebay.com for just $14.99 each.

These are your rooms, your sanctuaries, your retreats—to enjoy alone or share with someone special. Bedrooms and bathrooms should be restful, but they don't have to be dull or dated. Give your sleepy abode a wakeup call with the lively, low-cost ideas in this chapter.

FOCUS ON THE BED A creative headboard can become a fabulous focal point. Mat and frame pictures you already own, or download some from the Web. See directions *below.*

budget themes for bedrooms

Staying within a budget—even a $50 one—doesn't mean you have to settle for blah decorating. Here are some decor hints that will help you add star style for less:

- **Go Eurostyle.** Pick a fabulous border—Parisian street scenes or the canals of Venice (about $25 for two rolls). Sponge-paint the walls coordinating colors with one to two gallons of paint (less than $24). *(See how to sponge paint in Chapter 4.)*
- **Introduce Asian.** Associated with pared-down bedrooms, this style is still thriving. The payoff for the budget minded: fewer pieces of furniture and a bare minimum of accessories.

- **Tango with the tropical.** A few tropical accessories, such as animal-print window treatments, wicker chests, and bamboo curtain rods, can liven up the tamest bedroom on the cheap.
- **Simplify with black and white.** If you like classic, sophisticated styles, this theme's for you. Paint your walls a creamy white (less than $30) and paint thrift shop tables, or tables you already have, black with a lacquer finish. For a dramatic headboard, grab black frames from the dollar store and fill them with copies of great black-and-white photos by Margaret Bourke-White, Henry Brisson, or Ansel Adams.

HOW TO
use photos as a headboard

1 Start with 4×6-inch snapshots you have, or download images from the Web.
2 Visit a crafts or hobby store for discount frames that coordinate with other pieces in the room.
3 Make mats from colored construction paper or poster board, rather than buy expensive mat boards and a mat cutter.

low-cost headboard ideas

No doubt about it, it's the first thing you notice. The star of the room. The focus. The mood setter. We're talking about the headboard, of course.

If you've checked out bedroom sets in furniture stores, you know how pricey headboards can be. That's why we've put together these great ideas that cost under $50. Not only are they easy on your pocketbook, they'll showcase your originality and reflect your personal decorating style.

- **Pressed-tin ceiling tiles** mounted as a headboard can give a room a romantic, cottage look that's truly unique. Look for them at salvage yards and junk shops.

- **Here's an incredibly easy,** stylish substitute for a high-end headboard. Choose several yards of material in a lovely color. Drape it in a square shape on the wall behind the head of your bed, attaching it with double-stick tape. Then mount elements you love on it. Ideas to try are a '40s-era mirror, watercolor sketch (no need to frame it), bejeweled shawl, or an ethereal bunch of baby's breath.

- **An odd number of old shutters** can form a headboard. Choose new ones and paint them the color that best suits your bedroom's look.

- **A unified feeling** comes from mismatched pieces such as a bed frame and small tables. Introduce colors with inexpensive linens and throw pillows.

HOW TO
make the picket fence headboard

1 **Purchase one picket fence section** at a home improvement center.
2 **Buy bolts** long enough to go through the panel and bed rail.
3 **Cut the panel** to the bed width.
4 **Sand off** rough spots as needed.
5 **Mark the positions** for the bolts on the panel to match the holes on the bed rail.
6 **Drill holes** for the bolts through the panel.
7 **Fasten the headboard** to the bed rail with bolts and washers.

FENCE IT IN Add a whimsical touch with the headboard, *below.* Just hang a length of picket fence behind the bed ($7–$19 for a 6×8 section at home improvement centers.) See how, *below.*

MAGIC WITH METAL
Three retro metal screen door inserts discovered at a salvage yard hang behind the bed, *far right,* to add pattern and interest.

don't get framed—thrifty wall art

Think outside the box. You don't need pricey, framed art from a furniture store to decorate your walls.

Rather, let your walls evolve as your decorating style emerges. Instead of humdrum floral or scenic pictures, try some of these ideas:

In main living spaces:
- A bright kimono
- Colorful road signs or maps
- Secondhand quilts (family heirlooms, if you're lucky!)
- Black-and-white family photos in various sizes and shapes

In your kitchen:
- Antique cooking tools (whisks, eggbeaters, butter molds, ladles, etc.)
- Fanciful aprons
- Farm implements

In a feminine bedroom:
- Three pastel lingerie pieces from the '40s-'50s (on padded hangers of pastel silk)
- A collection of hats
- Unusual purses in various sizes and shapes

In a masculine bedroom:
- A collection of men's hats
- Walking sticks of various sizes
- Vintage ties

In a child's room:
- A colorful collage of children's book covers
- Blocks of numbers or letters
- Board games with graphic patterns and bright colors

In your bathroom:
- Assorted seashells you've collected—"framed" by tiny white twinkle lights
- Various sizes of starfishes
- Natural reed beach mats (with fabric-bound edges) hung vertically side-by-side for a tropical look

caring for your quilts

Because hand-made quilts are so fragile, keep these care tips in mind:
- **Don't dry-clean quilts,** and launder them as little as possible. When they need to be washed, check with quilting or fabric shops to purchase laundry detergent formulated especially for quilts.
- **Wash quilts** in cool water on the gentle cycle. Dry on the low or air cycle.
- **When you display folded quilts,** rearrange and refold them often to avoid damage from light along the edges.
- **If you use a quilt as a coverlet** or folded on a bed, turn and rotate it for even wear.
- **If you hang a quilt as art** on the wall, use a proper quilt frame. Keep it out of direct light and turn it often for even wear.

LADDER WALL ART This gently worn ladder, *right,* is the perfect backdrop for hanging quilts because it fits the mood of the room. You can easily find a new one (and paint and age it) for less than $15 online at ebay.com. Or buy a used one for less than $25 at garage sales or farm auctions.

For a bedroom that's relaxing, minimized colors, patterns, and furnishings create serenity. When working with multiple spaces and closets, choose paint colors and surface finishes that unify the look. For halls and dressing rooms that receive little natural light, use white to visually expand the area.

wake up to color

Nothing affects how a room feels to you more than its color. Whether it's light and bright or high-voltage bold, color is your primary tool to create the mood you want. Here are some tips:

- **If you prefer a cheery room** with a sunny look, painting the ceiling to match the walls makes the room more cozy and inviting.
- **If you like neutral backgrounds** to showcase collectibles or a special piece of furniture, a monochromatic scheme might work for you. Putty, cream, raffia, gray, sand, celadon, khaki, and white all work. Slight variations in tones increase a sense of serene spaces.
- **Weave in an accent color** if you go for neutrals. That might be a brilliant blue, or even passionate purple. Color used in different ways is less predictable and can set your own personal style apart.
- **Choose wall colors that flow** easily from room to room. Soft natural colors, including browns, greens, terra-cotta, and gray-blues work well in a whole-house color scheme.
- **Add a bit of black.** Designers say almost every room benefits from the contrast.
- **Be bold.** Strong colors can define spaces for special uses, such as a dining nook or home office. Current favorites are tomato red, coral, lavender, periwinkle, and shades of pink.
- **Don't be afraid to paint your floors.** For example, to get a fresh, Scandinavian look, floors can be painted in light tones and patterns, then sealed with polyurethane for long-lasting wear. Light-starved rooms will benefit from off-white paint on floors.
- **If you like the farmhouse look,** combine all shades of white paint and muted colors. Browns, grays, creams, and whites can make up the palette. In this scenario, use paint with minimal gloss for a muted effect.

The chart below can help you choose the right color for the mood you want.

WARM AND VIVACIOUS Some like it hot. If that's your style, paint your bedroom with bold reds, pinks and yellows, like this room, *left.* Two gallons of interior paint (about how much you'll need to give an average bedroom two coats) will cost you about $30.

CREATE A FARMHOUSE FEELING Busy patterns and contrasting paint can get in the way of a pure-and-simple farmhouse scheme, *below.* If you want that style, warm up the room easily with bright paint for about $15.

Color	Mood
Taupes, browns, grays, whites	Quiet, calm, stable
Blues, greens	Restful, relaxing
Bold reds, pinks, yellows	Warm, sunny, high energy

HOT TIP

No time to sew? Don't even own a sewing machine? You can still make curtain panels and pillows using fusible hem tape. Layer strips of hem tape between folds of fabric. Follow the package directions, using a heated iron to activate the tape. Look for hem tape in the sewing aisle of discount stores and crafts stores.

discover your dream space

These tips will help you gather the right accessories, arrange your bedroom to meet your needs, and make you feel totally at ease in your retreat.

- **If you're the formal type,** you'll probably want to center your bed along a wall, or between two windows, and then put nightstands on both sides.
- **If you're into casual ambience,** try looser, asymmetrical room arrangements, such as moving the bed to one side of the room, or angling it headfirst into a corner.
- **If clean and simple describes your style,** comfort may mean paring everything down to beautiful basics. Start with an eye-grabbing bed frame, and keep accessories to a minimum. Go for closed storage to keep your sanctuary restful and clutter-free.

FINESSE WITH FABRIC If you have a canopy bed, use inexpensive sheer panels like the ones, *right,* to help frame it. You can find tabbed panels similar to this for $19.99 a pair online at bizrate.com.

USE CONTRASTING STRIPES Add a whimsical note by painting a chest one color, and then the fronts of the drawers in contrasting stripes, *above.* Paint for this project costs less than $20.

custom looks at discount prices

The clever homeowner of the bath *at the left* shares her low-cost decorating secrets. First, she shopped at her local home discount store for these bargains:

1. **Colorful sheets** to make the attractive shower curtain and window treatment.
2. **A matching pillow sham** that she used to create the rug.

Notice how the towels rolled up in the basket echo the colors of the sheets and rug for added drama.

Other great buys you can check out at home discount stores include:

- Stemware and glassware
- Casual dishware sets
- Quilts and bedspreads
- Towels and linens
- Framed artwork
- Window treatments
- Kitchen appliances, from toasters to cappuccino makers
- Artificial plants
- A variety of colors and sizes of candles
- Faux architectural elements, from cornices to columns
- Patio furniture and accessories

SHOWROOM STYLE Even small bedrooms and bathrooms such as the lavender and yellow bath, *left,* can sport custom designer looks with a thrifty set of sheets ($8–$12) and a pillow sham ($8–$15), from discount home stores.

THRIFTY SEATING In the bathroom with the yellow beadboard wall, the wooden chair (find similar ones online at ebay.com for $9.95–$30) takes up very little space. Yet it sets a relaxed, country mood.

in just an hour

Put your personal stamp of style in the bedroom and bath and make these spaces truly yours—for less cost and time than you'd ever think. For example, in just an hour or so you can:

- **Do a quick window treatment** by cutting wide sheer ribbons to various lengths. Tie one end of each ribbon to a seashell and the other around a thrifty tension rod.
- **Add more seating space quickly** by pinning colorful sheets over a battered chair or ottoman.
- **Make an impromptu nightstand** by covering a round hardboard table from a home discount store with a pretty tablecloth you already have.
- **Create a quick bedside table** with a country accent by putting an antique kid's wagon lengthwise at the side of the bed. You can use the inside for magazines, books, an alarm clock, or reading lamp.

SAVOR SIMPLICITY Gather stones and lilies or other flowers from your garden and arrange them on a small table with a vase for a simple, serene feel, *left.* Use a few books to lift important elements and you'll have a unique display—for no cost at all.

USE PLATES AS ART Watch for pretty plates at garage sales and flea markets ($5–$25 each) and hang them like artwork, such as the arrangement *below.*

HOT TIP

Other inexpensive items you can use to help create displays include:

- Colored or clear bottles and vases
- Assorted flea market alarm clocks of any era
- Photos in a variety of discount frames
- A collage of pastel paper fans

fun themes for kids' rooms

Let your teen help make the decorating decisions and he or she might even occasionally make the bed. Here are some ideas to get you two started discussing decorating schemes:

- **Starry, starry night**—perfect for the would-be astronomer or astronaut. Start by painting the walls a dark blue, then adding glow-in-the-dark stars or painting stencils of stars in a lighter color over the base.
- **Lavender and lace**—great for the teenage girl who goes for the feminine. Paint the walls a medium to light lavender and the woodwork white. Drape gauzy white lace casually over plain curtain rods for the window treatments.
- **Music lover's paradise**—use a medium blue for the walls and simple white miniblinds at the windows. Give music the starring role by framing CD covers (copied and enlarged) of your teen's favorite songsters. Add some interest with framed, vintage LPs.

DRAMATIZE YOUR DRESSER The painted plaid design, *left,* adds a whimsical note to what was a changing table. (A great example of adapting what you have for little money.) Fresh paint—about $30 for all the different colors—makes it come alive.

If there are ink and crayon marks or water stains on the surfaces to be painted, use a stain-blocking primer on the furniture piece prior to painting. This will prevent marks and stains from bleeding through the finished paint job.

paint furniture

Scratched, dented pieces of wood furniture are bargains ($10–$40) at garage sales and flea markets. With a little inspection and work, you can turn someone's trash into your decorative treasure.

1. **First inspect the piece** to see if it's just surface damage. If so, you could transform it with paint. If the damage is substantial, you might want to pass.
2. **Fill dents and holes** with wood filler; let dry.
3. **Lightly sand the entire piece;** wipe clean. (For layers of peeling paint, you may need to use a chemical stripper first. Follow manufacturer's directions.)
4. **Paint with a water-base primer;** let dry.
5. **Paint on a base coat** of color using latex paint; let dry.
6. **Apply designs freehand** or use painter's tape to mask off stripes for crisp edges. (For more intricate designs, use stencils or stamps.) Let dry.
7. **Protect your work** with two coats of clear, water-based polyurethane.
8. **Let sealer dry** thoroughly between coats.

HOW TO
paint a sky on walls and ceilings

Although this sky effect was done with wallpaper, you can achieve the same effect with the painting technique called ragging. Here's how:

1. **Start with a base coat** of sky blue and let dry.
2. **Add clouds** by dipping the end of a rag or a piece of household sponge in white paint and dabbing the paint on the walls.
3. **Use a clean dry rag** to blend and soften and create a look similar to the clouds in the photograph.
4. **Experiment** with this technique on poster board first until you achieve the look you want in your room. *(For more information on ragging, see Chapter 4.)*

thrifty kids' room decor

The neat thing about decorating kids' rooms is that you get to think like a kid all over again. So put away your watch, organizer, and 12-month planner and have some fun with these ideas perfect for the youngest in your family:

- Take a trip to your local Salvation Army or Disabled American Veterans (DAV) store. They often have sturdy infants' and children's furniture for under $50. You could paint them with bold, primary colors for a lively, dramatic kids' room.
- Let your child pick a favorite simple coloring book and paint some of the easiest pictures on the walls or furniture, using the book as a guide. Choose colorful hues for a one-of-a-kind look.
- Go slowly. If your child wants to decorate in the latest trend, limit those pieces to inexpensive ones like throw rugs, pillows, or lamp shades. That way, when the trend passes in a year or two, you won't be out major money.

For cute curtain ties in a baby's room, try:
- Pastel baby shoes wrapped around both sides of a curtain and tied together.
- Baby spoons. (You can even find decorative ones at the dollar store.) Just glue ribbon matching your decor to the back of the spoon, and tie the ribbon around the curtain with the spoon showing at the front.

BLUE SKIES This serene sanctuary, *opposite page*, recalls those worry-free days with fluffy painted clouds, perfect for children or adults. The treatment pictured uses wallpaper, which costs from $20–$47 for an average bedroom. But you can also get this effect with ragging. *(See instructions opposite.)*

CALLING ALL FIREFIGHTERS Transform closets into a faux locker room by painting bifold doors to look like locker doors, *above*. It costs only about $15 for the paint.

HOT TIP

If space allows, get a secondhand, overstuffed chair for your child's room and cover it with sheets or tablecloths that match the decor. You'll find it a comfy place for the two of you to cuddle for that bedtime story.

how to decorate with your kids

Letting your child help decorate their own room is a great way to have fun, let them express their personality, and even learn the value of budgeting. You could:

- **Look through magazines together**— women's and decorating ones are best— clipping out pictures that appeal to them.
- **Choose several colors** that will work well in the room, using the pictures you've chosen. (You may need to point out that firehouse red or funky fuchsia on all the walls could get old fast.)
- **Decide your budget**—in this case, less than $50 and what you could do with it. Here are a few examples:

1. **Paint the walls.** ($15 for 1 gallon—the amount needed for most kids' rooms.)

2. **Create no-sew window treatments** ($12 for on-sale fabric or for valances only at a home discount store).

3. **Choose some of these** in the room's colors: accent rugs, bedside lamps, and wall art (about $5 each at garage sales and thrift shops such as Goodwill).

4. **Together,** paint, do window treatments, and maybe refurbish your thrift shop finds.

SEASIDE BOOKEND This sand-bucket bookend, *below,* adds fun to a bookshelf. Just fill a small plastic bucket ($2–$6 at home centers) with sand to give it weight, and tuck in a starfish ($3–$6 at crafts stores if you don't have one).

DOLLHOUSE DECOR As shown above the bed, *right,* you can display vintage kids' clothes ($5–$38 online at shockadelic.com or vintagetrends.com) in lieu of a headboard. Get an inexpensive shelf with pegs (about $12–$15 at home discount stores) for hanging these items.

where to forage for bargains

It's the lure of the unknown. The thrill of the chase. The uncovering of a special treasure surrounded by trash and trinkets.

We're talking flea market foraging. Junk shop junkets. Auction action. Don't limit your search for thrifty buys to home discount centers (although they have good prices too). Put on some comfy shoes, grab a friend and some bottled water and head for:

- Garage sales
- Junk shops
- Antique shops
- Specialty shops
- Auctions
- Yard sales
- Flea markets
- Import shops
- Liquidation outlets
- Consignment shops
- Salvation Army thrift shops
- Disabled American Veterans (DAV) thrift shops

- Goodwill thrift shops
- Other thrift shops operated by community groups such as the Junior Women's League, Friends of the Ballet, etc. You can probably call your local chamber of commerce to get a list of these, or possibly find out where to obtain a list.

HANG FARM IMPLEMENTS Here's a good example of using ordinary objects for unusual purposes. *At the left,* a corn planter wears its original red paint as a wall vase for flowers. Look for tools like this at outdoor auctions and antique flea markets for $6–$25.

TRY THRIFT SHOP PILLOWS Mix in these finds, *lower left,* with pillows you already own for a shot of color. Use a theme to tie the collection together, whether it's floral prints or a certain era. Shop online at ebay.com for vintage pillows from $4.95–$28.

USE YOUR TREASURES Here a mixture of old glasses, Mason jars, perfume atomizers, and other bottles, *above,* all found at flea markets for less than $30 total, proudly host a dainty harvest of blooms.

SHOW OFF COLLECTIONS A colorful collage of postcards, *left,* cost less than $25 at an antique store, and adds character to a guest room. Another collection shown is free from Mother Nature—an intriguing collage of attractive stones.

What's the secret to creating captivating windows? Simply these: Style, attitude, and unique design. From unusual low-cost rods to decorative hangers and tiebacks, you'll be amazed how easy dazzling window decor can be.

_You could jazz up your windows with faux animal prints. Use gauzy, pastel side panels and top treatments for a romantic feel. Choose colorful vintage fabrics for a touch of cottage chic. It's your imagination that's the star here, not your pocketbook.

For a fail-safe whole-house window treatment plan, mix and match only two or three classic styles throughout your entire home. Try drapery panels and blinds combined with fabric valances that match your furnishings. If your window styles and sizes vary within a room, use the same fabric for various window treatments, such as a valance topping a shade or the same fabric in long panels.

VOTE FOR VINTAGE This old tablecloth makes a cheerful topper. Bright designs from the '40s and '50s make super valances. Look for bargain linens at garage sales, junk shops and farm auctions for $5–$35.

here's where to start

The right window treatment can transform a flawed space into something beautiful that reflects your personal style. It can highlight a room's good qualities, or turn problem areas into sleek, sophisticated seating spaces.

But before you begin choosing your window treatments, consider:

- **Needs for privacy** and energy control. Gauzy swags may be beautiful with your wicker guest room, but you may need shades beneath them for better insulation.
- **The amount of light you want** through your windows. If privacy isn't an issue, choose top treatments, such as interesting valances, alone.
- **Traffic patterns.** Puddles of silk flowing from a dining room window add great atmosphere, but they wouldn't be practical for a sliding patio door.
- **The wall colors,** furnishings, and floor coverings in each room, so the window treatments work well with them.
- **Windows you want to highlight.** Ones with the best views or the most interesting architecture deserve the most striking, unusual treatments.
- **Thrifty miniblinds** and shades for strictly functional windows.

SHINE ON A faux-silk scarf (approximately 20×90) adds sheer elegance to this window, *left.* Buy them at women's consignment shops or online at ebay.com for $5–$25. The scarf can also double as a window valance when hung by pierced earrings, *right,* on wall hooks. Look in dollar stores for pierced earrings to match your color scheme.

HOW TO
create this scarf treatment

1. **Place wall hooks** into the trim above the window.
2. **Measure the distance** between the hooks and add 4 inches to create the swagged look. Divide this amount in half.
3. **With an equal length of fabric,** starting at the center of the top edge of the scarf, measure out the distance in step 2. Sew the earrings at these points and hang them from the hooks.

low-cost solutions for sun and privacy

Shutters, shades, and blinds all come in different colors, styles, sizes, and materials. But they all fill the same practical roles—light control and privacy. Here are some tips for choosing the best solutions without depleting your pocketbook:

- **If you like a simple,** minimalist look, go for inexpensive shades that can be rolled or pulled up and out of sight.
- **Thrifty miniblinds** are great for kids' rooms. Special bonus: they come in decorator colors at no extra cost. Just make sure cords are properly installed, tucked away, and well out of reach of your children.
- **If your home is fairly new,** heat loss and gain through your windows may not be an issue because many of today's windows are energy efficient. You could probably get by with cheaper blinds that don't conserve energy as much as the high-end ones.
- **Try topping drafty, older windows** with a treatment featuring wool or velvet. These fabrics offer thermal insulation, and can be bought for a song on sale at fabric stores and discount centers. They should help guard drafty windows against energy loss. (Just avoid this treatment if you want to make your room look bigger, as they tend to "shrink" a room.)

BRANCH OUT This simple styling uses branches you gather outside as curtain rods for no cost. Find tab-topped sheer panels on sale at home centers—or at $19.99 per set of two panels online at smartbargains.com.

HOT TIP

If your room is small, help it seem larger with window treatments. To add height, install curtain rods near the top of the room, rather than on the window frame. This draws attention toward the ceiling. Buy longer curtains if you do this. Avoid complicated or heavy fabric valances laden with trim if you want your room to seem larger—these can make windows seem smaller.

HOW TO
do this simple treatment

1. **Collect a long, narrow branch** that can be trimmed to fit your windows
2. **Use plant-hanging hooks** to fasten the branch rods to the ceiling or window frame.
3. **Tie spaghetti-strap or tabbed, sheer panels** from the central section of the branch.
4. **Collect beautiful stones** outdoors that have a pleasing color and shape for the room.
5. **Use stones** as anchors to keep panel from blowing in the breeze.

call it casual

BE A STAR Instead of a ho-hum rod, try stickpins (4 for $1 at many dollar stores) as drapery hardware, *left*. Just top a small, sheer scarf ($10–$20 at women's consignment shops or discount stores) slightly larger than your window with pins at upper corners. Then sweep a bottom corner to the window sash on the other side and pin it to the frame.

PEG SOME STYLE White Shaker pegs (6 for $2.95 at home improvement stores) add a welcome country touch to this refreshing blue-and-white window treatment, *below*. Find a similar valance at home stores for $8–$15.

Light and airy window treatments, such as the look *at the left,* are perfect companions to casual living. Using simple window treatments like this help keep the focus on the architectural aspects of your home, your furnishings, or the view outside.

A simple, pared-down look is more popular than ever, and it goes hand in hand with informal styling. Plus, there's a double bonus for you with this look: It's thrifty and easy to do yourself.

You can easily hide unattractive views—an unsightly neighbor's garage or a parking lot—with the right window treatments. Just add sheers, the more opaque the better. Or use blinds, shutters, or shades. Carefully position the blinds, shutter slats, or louvers to maximize light and obscure unappealing views.

HOW TO
do the shaker peg treatment:

1. **Find Shaker pegs** in the dowel section of a home discount or home improvement store.
2. **Hang a curtain valance.** Mark the points for the pegs on the window frame, placing one at each end and spacing the others evenly, about 6 inches apart. Note: if you don't want to drill directly into your window frame, cut a board to fit over the frame, and screw it in place.
3. **Space holes.** Drill a hole to receive the peg at each marked point. Glue the pegs in place
4. **Tie on a valance** or full-length curtain panel to finish the look.

7 steps to winning windows

Magical makeovers can change windows' appearance and minimize flaws. Here are some top tips:

1. Make narrow windows look wider by extending draperies or shades several inches on either side. Give a wide window height by starting window treatments above the frame.

2. Help a group of smaller windows seem unified with a single treatment—-it also will make the room seem larger.

3. Make two adjacent windows look larger and more like a pair. For each, do a single drapery panel pulled back in the opposite direction.

4. For different-shaped and -sized windows, hang drapery rods or valances at the same height to make windows appear the same.

5. Pull narrow window casements together with one graceful swag valance. If casements are in a corner, dress each side window separately.

6. Think BIG for small windows. A window less than 2 feet across can look wider. Just use curtains and a dramatic cornice hung outside the casement.

7. Make small rooms look larger. Choose small patterns in fabrics. Try low-contrast geometric patterns, tone-on-tone checks, or ticking for appealing treatments. Instead of large, busy prints in the window coverings, add large-scale focal points in contrasting pillows, borders, or wall prints.

INSTANT CHARM Top a child's bedroom window, *right*, with a simple shelf ($15–$25 at home improvement centers) to display dolls, toy soldiers, and stuffed animals.

BEACH WHIMSY A fun room, like the beach-themed one *below*, benefits from a light, full-swoop window treatment. Formal rooms, such as dining rooms, easily pull off heavier, less flowy window treatments.

HOT TIP

Originally valances were used to conceal window hardware. Now they tie together windows of many styles, shapes, and sizes. For a casual feeling, choose valances of light, sheer fabric, or a medium-weight fabric with a small print or checks. For a more formal feel, such as in a dining room, pick heavier weight fabrics.

HOW TO
swathe it in pink

Yards of opaque pink fabric can be hand-detailed with beaded strands to create a soft, romantic look:

1. **Measure your window** vertically and horizontally.
2. **Purchase opaque, pink fabric** at your fabric store. Make sure it's the same length as your window, but 1½ times its width.
3. **Buy beads that coordinate** with the fabric. You might want to try various shades of pink, purple and blue. Buy a needle and thread that work with the beads.
4. **Thread the needle** and slide on one bead on at a time, tying a knot after each bead.
5. **Thread enough beads** to make each strand 2½ inches long.
6. **Sew the strands** at various widths apart, to both the top and bottom of the length of fabric.
7. **Double the fabric** over the curtain rod and adjust it so both the top and bottom beading show.
8. **Tack or pin the layers together** just under the rod so they don't slip and slide.

tie it together

Choose a window treatment that unifies the various elements in your bedroom and bathroom. The fabric should complement bed linens, upholstered furniture pieces, and the shower curtain.

For variety, emphasize one fabric color in the bedroom and another in the bathroom. This adds interest, yet ties them together.

If you're using sheer gauzy fabric, breezes can stir up the panels and rearrange your treatment. To stop this, place curtain weights (available at home centers) inside the hem pocket at each corner and at each vertical seam. This way, panels will hang more symmetrically.

DREAM A LITTLE DREAM This treatment is romantic, easy and thrifty. Just follow the directions, *opposite*. You can find similar gauzy material at fabric centers from $8–$14 for the total quantity needed. Beads run $1.07–$2 per pack at hobby and craft stores.

DOUBLE YOUR PLEASURE For the final step in this project, just double the fabric over the curtain rod, *below,* and adjust it so the beading shows at the top and the bottom.

Did you know even windowless rooms can benefit from window treatments? A current popular technique is to frame an oil painting or mural as if it's actually a view. Shop locally or online for wallpapers with beautiful murals just perfect for this purpose—whether you prefer a lush, green countryside or a canal in Venice. A bonus is that these murals cost little because it's such a small amount of wall space you need to cover.

thrifty no-sew ideas

If you think all do-it-yourself window treatments always involve sewing, here's good news: They don't. The ideas below are great ways to perk up your windows without sewing a stitch.

All you need is imagination, creativity, and a sense of fun. Better yet, each idea below is well under $50.

1. Use salvaged vintage shutters instead of fabric treatments. Hinge the operable shutters and then attach them to the window frame to close for daytime sun control or nighttime privacy.

2. Design interesting curtain rods from cup hooks hung from ceilings, or bamboo canes from a garden shop.

3. Use long roofing nails and rubber bands to turn no-sew valances from drab to dynamite. Place roofing nails in the walls near the upper corners of the windows and attach fabric or scarves in a bouffant style to define a room and dress up a window. Use two coordinating fabrics for even more flair. Simply insert tissue paper or bridal netting to pouf swags.

4. Create a casual, inviting feel by simply draping fabric over a standard curtain rod, letting both ends puddle loosely on the floor.

5. Try sink fixtures or drawer pulls for festive window treatments. Pre-drilled nail holes make it easy to screw distinctive hardware into the window trim. It's a great, thrifty way to add drama in no time flat.

CREATE COTTAGE CHIC Using decorative curtain rings ($9.99 for 7 at home stores) or clip-on earrings ($2–$6 a pair at flea markets) adds charm to the window, *left.* Handsome rods ($9.99–$19.99 at home stores or online at bizrate.com) complete this popular look.

If you love cottage chic and new farmhouse looks, try draping vintage linen napkins or handkerchiefs over a curtain rod as a valance. Shop flea markets and antique shows for ones that feature the same color or one complementary to your room's decor.

penny-wise window decorating

If you're watching your pennies, don't try to decorate the windows in your house all at once. It's more fun—and cheaper—to take your time, and let your style evolve with the other decorating you do. Try treating your windows in stages:

1. **Compile an idea file.** Go through decorating or women's magazines (you can pick them up at garage sales for a couple of dollars). Cut out pictures of the windows and treatments that appeal to you. Don't worry about logistics or possible costs—you're just looking for inspiration at this point.

2. **Start with the basics** by hanging blinds, shutters, or room-darkening shades in the bedrooms and baths.

3. **Add side and top** treatments, as your time and budget permits.

4. **Resist starting in public places,** so you can cover the necessary windows for privacy first (in the bathroom and kitchen).

5. **Go back to your idea file.** See if any of the treatments you like could work in your home with a little adaptation.

BRING ON THE BLUES The blues take on a new meaning when they apply to this ethereal treatment that evokes a serene feeling, *opposite*. See directions *below*.

duplicate this look

It's easy to have a blue-ribbon-winning window with these simple steps:

1. Buy **15 yards** of 2-inch-wide voile ribbon to match the blue fabric you're using for your window treatment.
2. **Cut the voile ribbon** into 10 strips, each measuring 1½ yards long.
3. **Attach the ribbon** at the top of a matching color panel at even intervals, forming a loop for hanging. Slip the loops over the rod.
4. **Tie loose knots** 6 inches from the long, loose ends of each ribbon.

HOT TIP

Romance your windows by using pastel, floral-print fabrics or gauzy pastel sheers, as pictured on these pages. If you use two floral patterns in one room, vary the print size and choose patterns that use the same color palette to unify the total look.

It's low-cost, available in hundreds of hues, and able to change an entire room's looks in a twinkling. Paint is the affordable tool you need to totally transform any space. Whether you're aiming for a rich, formal look in your dining room or a casual feel for the den, you'll discover techniques to give you the exact look you want.

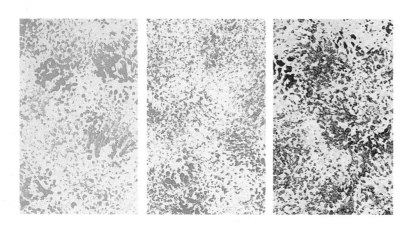

special effects

Sponging color on walls is an easy and fun way to experiment with techniques. Even beginners can achieve beautiful results like the wispy clouds of blue and yellow above the fireplace, *right*.

VARY THE INTENSITY You can intensify the color by using more paint on your sponge—from a very light, *far left*, application to a heavy one, *near left*.

HOW TO
sponge paint

1. Select two to three colors of paint.
2. Roll on the base coat; let dry.
3. Use a natural sea sponge, household sponge, sponging mitt, or any of the materials, *right*, to apply color top coats.
4. Wet the sponge; squeeze out excess water. (When using applicators such as cheesecloth, burlap, or brown paper, *right,* loosely wad the material, then wet and wring it.)
5. Dip the applicator into the paint; blot the excess off onto paper towels.
6. Lightly press the applicator onto the surface, allowing some base coat color to show through.
7. Reposition and turn the applicator to avoid repeating the pattern.
8. Repeat the process until the surface is covered as desired.
9. For a multicolor treatment, randomly sponge on one or two more colors in the same manner.

LOW-COST COLOR About $35 in paint and your own creative touch can achieve beautiful looks like the sponging in this living room.

paint

1. **Plan your decorative painting projects** when you have several consecutive days to work on them. While individual steps can be done quickly, overall processes may take time. Repair and wash your walls before you paint, if necessary.

2. **Read paint can labels** to estimate the amount of paint needed. Some cans of paint cover 300 square feet of painted wall, while some specialty paints cover only half that much. (You'll usually need only half as much glaze as you would of regular paint.) Try to get help if you're painting more than small wall sections. Larger areas are much easier when done with a partner.

3. **Keep a supply of drop cloths** and clean rags for protection and cleanup.

4. **When using rags** for applications or paint removal in techniques such as ragging or sponging, use the same kind of rag throughout the whole project so you'll get a consistent effect. Make sure the rags are clean and lint-free.

5. **Get different effects with all-cotton rags** than with blended or synthetic fiber rags. Try out the rag, paint, and selected technique first on a board to make sure you like the look.

6. **Consider the effects** of humidity on your painting. If you're working on a muggy summer day, you'll need more drying time than on a dry winter day.

7. **Step back from the wall** several times during each technique to look at the wall as a whole and get a sense of composition.

8. **Take out furnishings** or push them to the center; cover with drop cloths.

9. **Remove the outlet and switchplate covers** and anything on the walls. Use a putty knife to fill nail holes with surface compound; let dry. Lightly sand filled spots and vacuum up sanding dust. Wipe all moldings with a tack cloth to remove dust.

no-cost tips to get you started

Properly prepare the room before painting and use the right techniques for a beautiful finish. With the tips below and a change of tools, you can do striping, combing, ragging, and sponging in both casual rooms and more elegant ones.

CHOOSE THE BEST ROLLERS Good roller frames, *below,* have a compression-type cage with easily removed covers. Natural fiber roller covers are good for oil-base paints, varnish, or stains. Synthetic fiber roller covers are best for latex paints.

PROTECT YOUR WOODWORK Apply low-tack, quick-release painter's tape, *right,* where moldings meet the walls. It's easy to remove, won't leave a sticky residue, and is only $3 a roll at paint or hardware stores.

GET QUALITY BRUSHES Choose flat bristles for general painting and angled bristles for trim. To determine the quality, tug on the bristles. If more than two bristles come out, don't buy it. You'll need to pay $6–$7 in paint stores or home centers for a high-performance brush.

dress it in denim

As comfy and casual as your favorite jeans, this painting technique lets you give walls (and even furniture) the textural look of denim. Consider the faux denim technique if you want to create a relaxed atmosphere, such as in the bedroom, family room, or den.

Though blue denim is the most popular, you can get a denim-look finish in red or green. In the bathroom, *right,* cobalt blue stands out behind white fixtures. The distinct woven pattern is ideal for adding interest to an otherwise humdrum space.

why choose the blues?

In azure skies and aquamarine water, hyacinths and forget-me-nots, blue is the color Mother Nature loves. Although styles change through the years, a tasteful hue of blue is timeless. In Western culture and literature, blue has the reputation of creating a cheerful mood.

Blue is considered a cool color. It helps calm you down, rest your nerves, lift your spirits, and is generally soothing. No wonder it's so popular in private areas of homes, such as bedrooms and bathrooms.

GO AUTHENTIC For an even more realistic fabric look, add "seams" by overlapping painted sections slightly, like shown *at right.* The denim technique, which costs only about $35 for both the glaze and paint, is explained *on page 77.*

HOT TIP

Whatever the age and style of your home, consider your whole house when you plan your color and paint finishing schemes. Don't get carried away and use too many decorative painting techniques, such as ragging or sponging, in your home. Keep some rooms neutral or with plain paint to provide variety and help rest the eye. Unique painting techniques are great for smaller rooms like kitchens or baths, where the effect tends not to be overwhelming, as it could in a larger space.

doin' denim

The fine woven detail in this denim finish may look difficult, but with the right tools and a little patience, you'll get great results.

Because you'll use a liquid glazing medium, which dries fast, it's best to work in small sections at a time, or with a partner. What works: Your partner helps you with this project this time, you help your partner with his or her home improvement project later.

HOW TO
get this denim look

Materials and Tools
- White satin or semigloss latex paint for the base coat
- Satin or semigloss latex paint for the top coat in the desired color
- Glaze
- Painter's tape
- Roller and paint tray
- Weaver brush, *above*
- Lint-free cloth

1 **Paint the walls** with white latex paint; let dry.
2 **Divide the room** into vertical sections. Make them narrow enough so that you can work the sections from top to bottom quickly, but not so narrow that you can create more "seams" than are visually pleasing.
3 **Mask off alternating sections** with painter's tape. Mix 1 part glaze to 3 parts top coat paint.
4 **Roll the glaze/paint mixture** onto one section of the wall. While the glaze is still wet, stroke the weaver brush, *above,* down the entire section vertically and then across it horizontally.
5 **Wipe the brush with a lint-free cloth** after each stroke to remove excess glaze.
6 **Repeat the process** for every masked-off (alternating) section.
7 **Remove the tape;** let dry.
8 **Mask off** each unpainted section, positioning the tape ⅜ inch inside the edges of previously painted sections.
9 **Paint sections** with glaze/paint mixture in same manner as 5 and 6, painting over the ⅜-inch sections to create "seams." Remove tape; let dry.

One of the easiest ways to choose a color scheme is to copy some of the colors in a favorite fabric, such as this valance on the opposite page. Textiles are designed by professionals who know all about color. If you like the fabric, you'll probably feel comfortable in a room decorated from the same palette.

COORDINATE FABRICS
The colors in this valance, *opposite*, mix perfectly with a denim look.

comb it pretty

Move up in the style ranks when you decorate walls with this combing technique. It adds both drama and texture, so it's a good finish for rooms with slightly flawed walls.

going for green

Green is the color of rejuvenation, new growth, and promise. It has the ability to revive, and also to soothe. In general, yellowish shades of green, as shown here, are more stimulating, and blue-toned greens are more calming.

COMB THROUGH THE GLAZE You'll need a combing tool, *left,* to comb through the glaze while it's wet.

COMB IT CASUAL The informal look of combing, with its touchable texture, goes perfectly in comfy spots like dens, *right,* or family rooms.

HOT TIP

Although you're eager to get started, it's important to test your technique first. Whether you try it on an inconspicuous corner of the wall or on a separate board, you need to make sure the technique is going to give you the look you want. Ideally, wait 24 hours and check the test when it's dry.

HOW TO
master this technique

Materials and Tools
- Satin or semigloss latex paints in two closely related shades
- Painter's tape
- Glaze
- Roller and paint tray
- Crafts knife
- Wall comb

1 **Brush on the base coat** of paint; let dry.
2 **Mix the glaze and the paint;** the ratio depends on the depth of color you want. (The more glaze you use, the more sheer the color will be.)
3 **Test your mixture**—roll a small amount of glaze onto a wall in an inconspicuous area and drag the comb through it.
4 **Add more glazing** if the mixture is thick and leaves too much paint.
5 **With a damp rag,** remove the test glaze while the mixture is wet. Roll a section of the wall with the glaze mixture.
6 **Comb through the glaze** with a combing tool, *above.* Apply even pressure to help keep the lines straight.
7 **Wipe excess glaze** from the comb with a lint-free rag.
8 **If you end up in a corner** where the remaining area is smaller than the combing tool, use a small brush to paint back slightly into the area already combed to accommodate the width of the comb.
9 **Comb adjacent walls** on different days. Or, if combed on the same day, allow at least four hours between painting adjacent walls to avoid smudging.

whitewash for charm

White paint diluted with water transforms plain wood into a beguiling decorative element. When you think cottage-style, you may envision a weathered white or very light colored finish over tongue-and-groove panels, as shown in the living room, *below,* or beadboard, such as in the child's fanciful bedroom, *left.*

Creating this uneven painted finish is called whitewashing, pickling, or liming.

TAKE A FREE CLASS
Many home improvement centers offer free classes in painting techniques, from ragging and sponging to the whitewashing effects *shown on these pages.* Give local stores a call for schedules.

HOW TO
get this look

1. **Sand the entire surface** and wipe clean.
2. **Mix 2 parts white latex paint to 1 part water** in a container.
3. **Apply diluted paint** to surface, working quickly. Continue applying the paint/water mixture until the entire surface is covered. Let dry.
4. **For a more weathered, rustic look,** work in smaller sections and remove some of the paint before it dries.
5. **Use a clean, lint-free cloth** to wipe the surface and reveal more grain.

Colorwashing is
perfect to use on
walls that aren't in
great condition: Its
appearance helps
hide faults, turning
rough, inconsistent
walls into a surface
rich with color.

colorwash for drama

A great way to create a room that feels like a heavenly escape is to soften it with the ethereal look of colorwashing. It's a subtle effect, and yet can produce dramatic results.

If you're a free spirit, you'll especially love the process of colorwashing, which usually begins with paint diluted with either water or glaze. It's a great faux painting project for beginners because it's not very complicated or messy, and doesn't overpower a room.

Experiment with the technique *on the following pages,* applying the paint with a variety of different tools, such as brushes, rags, or sponges. A brush will leave lines in the finish for a textured look, while a sponge or cloth will create a softer appearance.

The recommended ratio is 4 parts paint to 1 part glaze or water, but you can adjust the mix to increase or decrease the translucency.

RETREAT AND RELAX The deep blues used for the colorwashing effect in this bedroom, *left,* create a feeling of ease and serenity.

add a splash of color

Colorwashing looks dreamy and gives rooms depth. That's because your eye looks through the glaze to the base coat below.

Adding glaze, rather than water, to the paint makes the color richer. But you can use either one. You can apply a colorwash over nearly any base coat color, but light to medium colors work best.

The glaze-and-paint or water-and-paint mixture will have more depth—from light to dark—when applied over a light color. You can also use colorwashing on furnishings and other objects to give them a fresh, new look.

ADD SOME IMPACT The two views of this bedroom, *below left,* show how colorwashing adds dramatic impact, and yet coordinates with other furniture and accessories for a unified look.

CHOOSING THE BASE It's best to select a light color for the base coat, such as the off-white, *upper left.* Here the homeowner chose blue for the top coat, which consists of adding glaze or water to the paint.

colorwash

Materials and Tools
- Satin or semigloss latex paint for the top coat in the desired color
- Latex glaze
- Water
- Paintbrush or roller and paint tray
- Bucket and mixing tool
- Application tool, such as a sea sponge, rag, or brush

1. **Mix the glaze—or water—and top coat** paint in the desired ratio. (A standard ratio for this technique is 1 part glaze or water to 4 parts paint.) Add water (even if you're using glaze) for more translucency.
2. **If using a sea sponge or rag,** apply glaze and paint or water and paint mixture to a 4-foot square section, rubbing it in a circular or figure-eight motion.
3. **If using a brush or similar tool,** apply the mixture to the wall in a crosshatching "X" motion. When using a brush in a crosshatching motion, all brushstrokes will be seen. If you are painting on a smooth wall, the more textured the wall, the less noticeable the brushstrokes will be.
4. **After the 4-foot section is complete,** immediately begin applying the glaze/paint mixture in an adjacent 4-foot section.
5. **Blend and smooth areas** between sections while the previous section is still wet and workable. Continue the process until the entire wall is complete.

If you're new to the painting techniques in this chapter, you may want to try one in a small room first, such as a bath or powder room. These smaller rooms come to life with painted color and pattern. And you won't be overwhelmed by having large surfaces to cover.

write a winner

A wonderful way to express your personality is to use words, phrases, or quotes in your decorating scheme. Calligraphy letters are beautiful—from graceful and flowing to bold and substantial. You can use this technique on walls, ceilings, floors, and furnishings.

You can apply calligraphy freehand, such as the fluid French cursive writing in the bathroom, *left*. The purple writing starts around the mirror. Then, for interest, some sayings are painted smaller and in a lighter color, while others flow onto adjacent walls.

It's even easier to create words using stencils. If you aren't doing a free-flowing design, keep your writings straight by drawing a baseline with a pencil and a carpenter's level. To keep letter heights uniform, draw a second line above the baseline at the desired height.

PLAYFUL OR SOPHISTICATED One of the benefits of calligraphy is its flexibility. It can be either whimsical, *left,* or elegant, *right*.

USE A STENCIL If you're new to calligraphy, it's easiest to trace a stencil on the wall for your first project. *(Instructions are on pages 88–89.)* You can find stencils in all kinds of styles in most art, hobby, and craft stores for $7 or less.

If you're a beginner with calligraphy, you may want to practice on some smaller crafts before you tackle a wall in your home. Art and craft stores have inexpensive supplies to make bookmarks, plant markers, T-shirts, and more.

letter perfect

You'll find a variety of tools to apply lettering, such as the paint, permanent, and calligraphy markers *shown here.* Or, try the carbon copy paper method, *below*, to easily transfer lettering you find in books or download from the Web.

HOW TO
create calligraphy

Materials and Tools
- Latex paint for the base coat in the desired color and finish
- Acrylic paint, paint markers, or permanent markers in desired colors
- Carbon copy paper
- Pencil

1. **Apply the base coat** to the surface; let dry.
2. **Select words or sayings.** Decide if you're going to write it yourself or use a font from a computer program. If you use a computer, choose a font, auditioning different sizes, and print the words onto the paper.
3. **Decide where you want** the letters.
4. **Place the paper** with the carbon side toward the surface. Lay type over the carbon paper and trace over the letter outlines with a pencil. Press hard to ensure the letters are transferred onto the project surface.
5. **Lift away the carbon paper** and fill in the outlined letters with acrylic paint and an artist's paintbrush, or with paint or permanent markers.

RSTUVWXYZ

MIX IT UP Don't forget about writing on furniture too. Here calligraphy dresses up a chest of drawers and wall surfaces.

ADD A PERSONAL TOUCH Although using a stencil or carbon paper might be easier, your own handwriting adds one-of-a-kind personality and a touch your kids won't soon forget, like shown on the dresser *below*.

choose colors
with confidence

Are you ready to lavish rooms with color? Use these tips to build up your courage and pick the perfect palette the first time around.

- **Establish the mood.** If you long for restful, choose pale blues and greens. If you want an invigorating feel, pick lively colors, such as bold red and purple.
- **Start with the furnishings.** Select key items in the room, such as an upholstered chair or painting, and build from there.
- **Vary the look.** Pair paint colors with items in the room, but don't match them exactly. Using the color you've chosen for the walls for accessories too may detract from them.
- **Shop prepared.** Take a fabric swatch, carpet sample, or even a piece of art when you shop for paint.
- **Collect paint cards** from paint or home improvement stores and take them home to see how they'll look in your room.

what affects color

As you get ready to add sparkle and spirit to your rooms with paint, you'll want to remember these principles that affect the shade you've chosen:

- **Drying time changes color.** Paint dries darker than it appears when wet.
- **Light changes color.** Note how your paint cards look in both natural and artificial light, as well as in the mornings and evenings.
- **Sheen changes color.** The shinier the finish, the lighter it will look.
- **Texture affects color.** Smooth surfaces reflect light, so a heavily textured wall will appear darker than a smooth one in the same color.

HOT HOT HOT Don't automatically shy away from bold colors when you do painting techniques such as the ragging in this bright orange kitchen, *left*.

BE INSPIRED Use a fabric to decide the colors for a room, *below*. Bring the fabric inspiration along when buying paint.

rag a rich finish

If you loved finger-painting as a kid, you'll delight in the freedom of ragging.

For this technique, the paint and glaze colors should complement each other. The closer the value of the colors, the softer the look. The greater the variation of colors, the stronger the pattern will appear.

For a traditional feel, consider ragging color onto stripes, such as in the bathroom, *left.* Here rich alternating stripes of cream and ragged on mocha are perfect with the clean white sinks and marble floor.

The basic tool you'll need is a clean, soft, lint-free cloth. Two values of the same color will produce a subtle, blended look while contrasting colors provide dramatic finishes.

See the directions for rag on and rag off techniques on page 95.

GO AGAINST THE GRAIN If you want a treatment that says something, don't just rag your walls—rag clean stripes for an elegant effect, such as in the bathroom, *left.*

For a subtle look, use a rolled rag instead of a wadded one. Dip the rag into a 4 parts paint to 1 part glaze mixture, roll it into a sausage-like cylinder, and gently roll it over wall.

from subtle to bold

It's easy to create dramatically different looks with two kinds of ragging. Ragging on is using a glaze/paint mixture applied to the wall or other surface with a rag, and can add bold impact to any room.

Ragging off is using a glaze/paint mixture applied to the wall with a brush or roller and then partially removed with a rag. It creates a more subtle color effect than ragging on.

DO A LOT WITH A LITTLE With a small amount of wall space, the rag on and rag off techniques used *at left* pack a huge punch.

rag on

1 Apply the base coat to surface; let dry.
2 Mix 4 parts of paint to 1 part glaze.
3 Dampen a cloth with water, wring out completely.
4 Dip the cloth into the glaze/paint mixture and wring out slightly.
5 Wad up the cloth so it has an uneven surface.
6 Apply the glaze/paint mixture to the wall, allowing some base coat color to show through.
7 Reposition and turn the cloth to avoid repeating the pattern. Use light pressure, or you'll get too much glaze on the wall and not enough pattern.
8 Repeat the process until each wall is covered.

rag off

1 Apply the base coat to surface; let dry.
2 Mix 4 parts of paint to 1 part glaze.
3 Apply the paint/glaze mixture onto an approximate 4-foot square section of the wall with the brush or roller.
4 Wad up the cloth so it has an uneven surface.
5 Press the cloth onto the wall, pouncing and wiping it to remove some of the paint/glaze mixture, exposing some base coat.
6 Reposition and turn the cloth to avoid repeating pattern.
7 Repeat the process, working in approximate 4-foot square sections. Let one wall dry completely before starting the next so you don't smudge corners.

HOT TIP

Ragging works well for smooth or textured walls. It's rather messy, so have lots of clean rags and drop cloths handy. Half of a clean, cotton T-shirt, with the sleeves, neck and hem removed, works well for this application.

Little things do count. It's the small details—from lamps to accessories—that sparkle up a room. In these pages, you'll see how to use them to create your special style—without breaking the bank.

If you're a diamonds-kind-of decorator on a costume-jewelry budget, take heart. These easy ideas, such as beautifying old lamps and rockin' with retro pillows—are so stylish no one will know you didn't splurge.

HOW TO
update a ginger jar lamp

1 **Apply hot glue** to an unglazed or sanded ginger jar lamp base.
2 **Wind sisal rope** in a spiral around the base of the lamp, beginning at the bottom.
3 **Work in small sections** so the glue doesn't harden too soon. (Or recruit a partner to help you.)
4 **Use one long piece** of rope (this lamp required 100 feet of ½-inch-diameter rope) to avoid having to piece sections.

WRAP SESSION This old ginger jar lamp ($5–$10 at garage sales and thrift shops) takes on a new look wrapped in sisal rope (just $11.96 for 100 feet at home improvement stores).

use-what-you-have decorating—for free

Part of the fun of creating your personal style is using what you already have—in a different style. You can train your eye to look at things in new ways, and use the unexpected to add a touch of color or whimsy. Best of all, it costs you nothing. Here are some ideas to get you going:

- Move the furniture around in a room. It doesn't cost a penny and you'll be amazed at how placement can affect the overall mood. For example, turn the sofa at an angle, position a low table under a window, or set an overstuffed chair in a dull corner.
- Hang colorful scarves or shawls on a cup rack in your bedroom for a splash of fun.
- Get an old tacklebox, toolbox, or lunch box that's just taking up space and use it for a planter on your deck or patio.
- Try that extra or mis-matched chair in a guest room or bathroom to hold linens or towels that complement the room's decor.
- Make an old piece of metal or wooden fencing an interesting architectural element on a wall, or use it as an unusual fireplace screen. It can also function in place of a headboard in your bedroom.
- Get out extra bedspreads or rugs. Try hanging them over your bed's headboard for texture and color.

AGE IT ARTFULLY Here's how to add character to a room—without forking over antique-store prices. This wooden planter, *left,* is aged by rubbing off some paint for a timeworn look. You may find a similar one at thrift stores or garage sales for $10–$30. See the directions for aging it, *right.*

PARADE YOUR PURSES These vintage purses, *right,* find a perfect home dangling from a rack. Disabled American Veterans (DAV) or Goodwill shops may carry aged purses for $2–$15. To hang them, use a wooden peg-style cup rack (about $1–$4 at dollar stores).

HOW TO
make a distressed planter *(far left)*

1. Use steel wool or sandpaper to rub off paint in areas that would see the most wear, such as on corners.
2. Add more age with a few nicks or scrapes with a hammer.
3. Paint the piece the color you've chosen.
4. Use a rag to lightly remove wet paint from freshly brushed pieces.
5. Fill with grasses or similar plants for a surprising pop of color.

beautify with bamboo

This earthy, exotic material is popular for so many styles, including contemporary, tropical, and contemporary country. Using bamboo in lamps, accessories, or furnishings is a great way to add texture to a room furnished mainly with wood pieces.

More pluses? Bamboo pieces are long-lasting, and require minimal care. Every couple of months, wipe them down with a sponge dampened with sudsy water. Then wipe them with a sponge wrung out in clear water and dry. (Don't try to clean them by hosing them down.) A thin coat of liquid wax will restore the shine.

A NEW LOOK FOR PENNIES If you've got an outdated lamp, here's a thrifty way to give it a tropical accent. You'll need PVC pipe ($8), a lamp wiring kit ($7.45), and about 6 feet of sisal rope ($2) from a home improvement store. Add in 10 bamboo pieces ($2 each) from a crafts store and you have a handsome lamp for under $40. See the directions *below*.

HOW TO
make this bamboo lamp

1. Buy a 12×3-inch piece of PVC pipe in the plumbing section of a hardware store or home center; most stores will cut the pipe for you at no additional cost.
2. Paint the wooden base and PVC pipe to match the bamboo; let dry.
3. Drill a hole near the bottom of the PVC pipe for the lamp wiring and in the cap for the socket end.
4. Use a lamp wiring kit, available at home centers or lighting stores, to make a lamp, following manufacturer's instructions, running the wire through the PVC pipe and out the drilled hole near the bottom. Glue the base and cap in place.
5. Hot-glue bamboo pieces, available at crafts stores, around the PVC pipe, covering it completely.
6. For a decorative band, wrap sisal rope around the bamboo several times and knot it to hold in place.
7. Top the lamp with the shade of your choice. Wicker is shown here.

curb it—free decorating with tossed-out stuff

CHEAP THRILLS

Here's a great source of potential decorating items: The things people leave outside on their curbs for haulers or city maintenance folks to pick up.

In most cities, anyone is welcome to pick these up FREE, which saves dump fees. Here are some goodies others have found, along with their possible uses:

low-cost ways to light it up

This sea-glass lantern answers the call for creative chic on the cheap. See how to make it *below.*

And don't ever underestimate the decorating potential of candles. Today they come in a huge array of colors, styles, shapes, sizes, and scents. They're a great—and inexpensive—way to change the mood and feel of a room.

For instance, fall calls for burnt orange and restful greens in scents such as cinnamon and evergreen. Come spring, change to pastel pinks and orchids in sweet aromas such as rose and lavender.

Possible Free Item	Potential Decorating Use
Bamboo poles	Unique curtain rods.
Used sewing machine	Use the iron bottom as a base. Find pre-cut glass for the top at hobby or craft stores. Then use it as a coffee table.
Worn-out, paned window	Display family photos or various types of collages or collections on it.
Old suitcases	Glue together two to three suitcases with super glue, decoupage them with antique or current travel postcards and use as an end table or coffee table.
Colorful bedspreads with stains or ironing scorches on them	Launder, cut out damaged sections, and use fabric to cover worn-out pillows.

HOW TO
make this light

1. **Put a small clear-glass cylinder,** such as a vase or a tumbler, inside a larger one of the same height. (If you don't have two cylinders, buy thrifty glass vases from a dollar store.)
2. **Place a votive** or tea light in the small cylinder. (You can find votive candles for 4 for $1 at most dollar stores.)
3. **Fill the space** between the two cylinders with clear or colored sea glass from a crafts store.
4. **Make several lanterns** and put them all around the area where you want to convey a soft, engaging ambience.

ADD A GLOW This sea-glass lantern adds sparkle to any deck. From a dollar store, get a large and a small vase ($3–$5 each) and a small votive candle (4 for $1). Add a bag of colored sea glass ($1.99 at hobby stores). These lights are so thrifty, you might want to make two or three—for yourself or to give to friends.

add stylish elements

One way to add instant character and interest is by displaying architectural elements. From worn gingerbread trim to iron fencing, these items dramatize your decor. Scour salvage yards, auctions, construction sites, or antique stores for pieces that catch your eye.

Remember, peeling paint and spots of rust are part of what make these pieces unique. You can even find inexpensive reproductions of salvage items—from medieval urns to faux marble columns—at import stores and home centers for under $50.

contrast textures

An important element of style is the juxtaposition of contrasting textures, such as the cool steel bowl, *left,* and the warmth of fresh pears. You'll discover gorgeous decorating bargains in the produce aisle of your local supermarket for a few dollars. The pastel pears are a creative alternative to pricey bouquets from a florist. Lemons, limes, and Granny Smith apples also work well.

ADD AN ELEMENT Nothing adds character as quickly as weathered architectural elements, *right.* Home discount stores offer a wide variety from $3–$40.

PICK PERFECT PEARS These pears ($1) in a bowl ($10–$25 at junk shops or garage sales), *above left,* add luscious color and shape to an arrangement.

HOT TIP

Did you know you can easily hang heavy items up to 50 pounds without having to use a wall stud? E-Z Anchors cost about $5 for a pack of 25 and are available at most home and hardware stores.

sprinkle in some whimsy

Pillows are the quick-change artists of decorating. Toss them around a room to add instant pattern or color, and then swap them out when you're ready for a new look. Here are a few tips on decorating with pillows:

- **If you're feeling creative,** buy plain decorating pillows ($5–$25 each at home discount stores). Then gussy them up with beads, tassels, or ribbons for a designer look without the designer price tag.
- **To make thrifty vintage pillows,** shop garage sales and secondhand stores for old yardage, tablecloths, quilts, or napkins. Snip away worn or soiled spots, launder, and use the rest for pillow covers with a lively retro flair.

use decorative hardware

Another easy way to add a whimsical touch is with decorative hardware. Take a trip to your local home improvement store and you'll discover a brave new world of hardware, knobs, and pulls. Try sunflowers or daisies in the guest room, and fanciful animals in kids' rooms. Often, just a new coat of paint and some new hardware can enliven even the most tired furniture.

PILLOWS ADD PUNCH
Whether it's a '30s Indian print, or a '40s brocade, pillows, *left,* are thrifty ways to add style. Shop online at ebay.com for vintage pillows from $1–$35 each.

PUT ON NIFTY KNOBS It's a thrifty way to get a fresh look. Remove knobs and spray-paint. You can find plain knobs for about $2 and decorative ones for $3–$6 at home improvement stores.

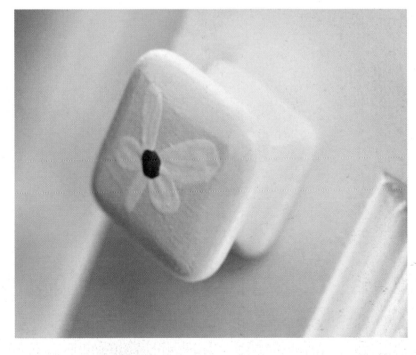

personalize your rooms with photos you have

Don't let the times of your—and your family's—life sit unused in dresser drawers or the attic. Photographs are a great, low-cost way to personalize your decor. Here are some quick suggestions to try:

- **Use a theme.** For example, take pictures of several generations' weddings and put them in various sizes of vintage frames to display in your dining room or bedroom. (Graduation pictures work well too.)
- **Got beach decor** going in the bathroom? Use a collage of your family's tropical vacations to decorate one wall.
- **Hang black-and-white family photos** in various sizes in an entryway or long hallway as a decorating element. Using all-black frames of varying materials (wood, papier-mâché, twigs) adds to the drama.
- **Lean a large family photo** against a wall on a mantel or tabletop, instead of hanging it. Then surround it with items of that era. For example, set '50s salt and pepper shakers around a snapshot of that era, or Victorian hankies around a photo of that vintage.
- **Copy an old family photo,** put it in a deep vintage frame, and use it for a vanity tray, or as a centerpiece with timeworn candleholders on top.

DANGLING ART For just $2.98 for the chain and $8 for the clips (both usually available at home discount centers) you can show off your photos with flair. See how *below*.

You should store your family photos in acid-free boxes or in acid-free mounts. A framed photo should have ultra-violet screening glass in front of it. Photos should be stored in a dark, dry, cool place for long life, so don't keep them in the attic or basement. The heat, damp, or cold can all damage them.

HOW TO
display photos from a chandelier

1 **String a lightweight chain** or beaded trim around the fixture.
2 **Use curtain ring clips** to suspend photos and postcards.
3 **Change the display** for the seasons. At Christmas, dangle photos of your family's past holidays. Pictures of your kids dressed as ghosts could take up residence around Halloween—you get the idea.

say it with windows

Often you can pick up weathered windows at farm auctions, estate sales, or junk shops for less than $50. With the glass taken out, they can become unique "frames" to display all your collectibles.

If you prefer a more finished look, you can sand, prime, and paint these pieces to match your decor, as in this living room *left*. Other ways to use windows are to:

- **Hang them as wall art** if they have an interesting shape or finish.
- **Use one as a "top"** for an improvised coffee or end table—if it doesn't have panes. For the base, get identical plant stands at a home discount store. Choose stands as tall as how high you want your table to be. Simply set the stands the desired distance apart and place the window on top. (Vintage doors work well for tops, too.)
- **Prop up an old window** for special occasions such as graduation, and glue on pictures of the graduate at various stages in his or her life. For more fun, attach a few report cards or comments from teachers.
- **Use large paned windows** from construction sites or salvage yards as room dividers to section off an eating or study area. They can be painted to coordinate with the room's decor.

WHAT A VIEW Sometimes other people's "junk" can be your treasure. You may find old windows free at the curb or at salvage yards and antique stores for $15–$50.

Make a small space look bigger by:

- Paring down furnishings with fewer, larger pieces.
- Using white walls and mirrors to help expand the space, with bold jolts of color as accents.
- Creating long sight lines from room to room by linking adjacent spaces with the same colors.

A deck, porch, or patio without your personal touch is little more than a slab made for sitting. Welcome to these simple projects that are easy on your pocketbook, but don't skimp on style.

You'll see how bringing that fresh-air feeling of the garden to outside living spaces makes them more inviting, and for far less than you might think.

HOT TIP

Make your fresh-cut blooms last longer by cutting the stems at an angle with a sharp blade. Remove any leaves that will fall below the water line. If possible, change the water and re-cut the stems every day. Use a floral preservative in the water. Your flowers will last longer if you keep them out of direct sunlight.

SHOWCASE YOUR BLOOMS To highlight flowers indoors, fill an antique wire milk carrier with wine carafes, *right*, or use vintage canning jars or milk bottles. You'll probably find wire carriers for $5–$15 at antique stores, and bottles from $1–$5 at garage sales and thrift shops.

HOW TO
create colorful pots and window boxes

1 **Buy plastic pots** and/or window boxes at a home discount center or dollar store.
2 **Use denatured alcohol** to wipe the surfaces (and saucers underneath, if any) to prepare them for painting.
3 **Spray paint containers** with terra-cotta color paint as a primer for the effect, *above*. (Try different colors, if you wish, that coordinate with other items in your setting.)
4 **Let the containers dry** thoroughly.
5 **To decorate them,** buy stencil patterns at a crafts or hobby store, and trace them on the planters with a pencil. (Or, if you're feeling crafty and creative, trace your own fun designs freehand.)
6 **Use enamel paint** and/or paint pens to decorate the exteriors.
7 **Protect your creations** with two coats of sealer, letting the first coat dry thoroughly before adding the second.
8 **Allow the last coat of sealer** to dry 24 hours before you add dirt or plants.

spotlight
fresh flowers

You and your family can enjoy nature in your outdoor living spaces with these creative ideas. For the patio or porch, thrifty plastic containers take on new style with the directions *below left*.

As a fast way to elevate a plant to focal point status, place it in a container in the birdbath, *below*. Leave it filled with water for the birds to enjoy.

PAINT THOSE POTS Visit the home discount center for plastic pots and window boxes from $2–$10 and spray paint for $3 a can. With stencils ($5) and paint pens ($2–$4) from a crafts stores, you can create pots with pizzazz. See directions, *opposite*.

IT'S FOR THE BIRDS Attract your feathered friends with a birdbath ($20–$40 at import stores or home centers). Chances are, they won't even notice the pot ($5–$10 at home centers) in the middle.

Line up pots and plants of all different sizes, colors, and dimensions to gently shape the outer edge of an outdoors living space. Remember that tall, slender planters can provide height, while shorter, wide pots leave a window-like opening for a spacious feeling. Best of all, these walls may be moved as your mood or the season changes.

frame a beautiful view

Every garden needs a special portal to reveal its true heart and soul. Visit your local salvage yard, flea market, garage sales, or thrift shops for wonderful vintage doors or windows under $50.

For example, the window, *left,* can spotlight a favorite scene. Twist eyebolts into the frame and into an overhang on the house. Hang the sash from the eaves with chain.

Entice guests into your garden with worn doors, *right,* still sporting old paint for a cottage garden look. You can even use just one door for the same effect. For a more formal garden, try a door or two with metalwork insets.

VINTAGE WOOD ADDS CHARM To most of today's designers, weathered wood adds charm to indoor and outdoor elements *pictured here.* You may find these at flea markets for $10–$45 or even free at the curbside. Leave them outside untreated for even more weathering.

No salvage yard handy? Call local remodeling or demolition firms and ask if they sell elements scrapped from old buildings.

use low-cost metal

Because metal stands up to most everything that Mother Nature throws its way, you can find many affordable weathered garden items for far less than you might imagine.

These watering cans take on a leading role when gathered atop an old barn bench and used as planters. For variety, include both painted and plain galvanized cans.

Try a wonderful, '50s retro-style metal chair like the one shown if it meets your budget and is sturdy.

MIX VINTAGE AND NEW Mixing the '50s chairs, *below,* and weathered watering cans, *left,* works well when the materials are alike (in this case, metal). Farm and garage sales can be gold mines for watering cans or vintage metal chairs, from $2–$35.

HOT TIP

When decorating outside living spaces, look for exterior-grade materials that are designed to withstand the elements. Metal ones, such as these pictured, tend to hold up well through the decades. To protect them, give them a coat of matte-finish marine varnish (available at hardware stores and home centers) for even longer wear.

thrifty outdoor lighting

The night sky is the most beautiful when its bejeweled in thousands of stars. Bring that enchanted glow down to earth with creative lighting for spirited evenings on your deck, patio, or other outdoor entertaining area. Here are some bright ideas that won't leave your wallet empty:

- **String colorful paper lanterns** to add an exotic feel to entertaining outdoors.
- **Use small votives,** flanked by candles of various heights, to provide shimmer.
- **Try tiny twinkling white lights** for a romantic glow. You may be able to find enough by raiding your stored boxes of Christmas decorations.
- **Add an exotic touch of the tropics** to any gathering with tall wicker or bamboo torches. You can pick them up for $5–$8, and the refills are $4–$5. Now you can even get citronella fuel, to help repel unwanted guests—mosquitoes and other bugs.

STRING THEM ALONG Try an import store for large paper lanterns (about $8–$12 each) or a strand of miniature ones (around $10) and add a touch of glamour to your outside living spaces.

ADD SOME SPARKLE Use floating candles
(4 for $1 for small ones, 2 for $1 for large
ones at dollar stores) to jazz up your
evenings. Or visit a home center to buy
twinkling white lights (just $4 a strand) to
nestle in small pots ($2 each) for an outdoors
garden feeling.

get your garden glowing

You don't have to be an expert crafter or carpenter to add a touch of glamour and excitement to your outdoor living areas. Here are just a few ideas:

- **Transform ordinary holiday lights** with garden-style shades made from tiny terra-cotta pots. See the directions *below*.
- **Take floating candles outdoors** by using a birdbath as a basin. Line the bottom with smooth river stones and add flower-shaped votive candles. Sprinkle in small blooms from your garden, light the candles, and see how your garden glows.

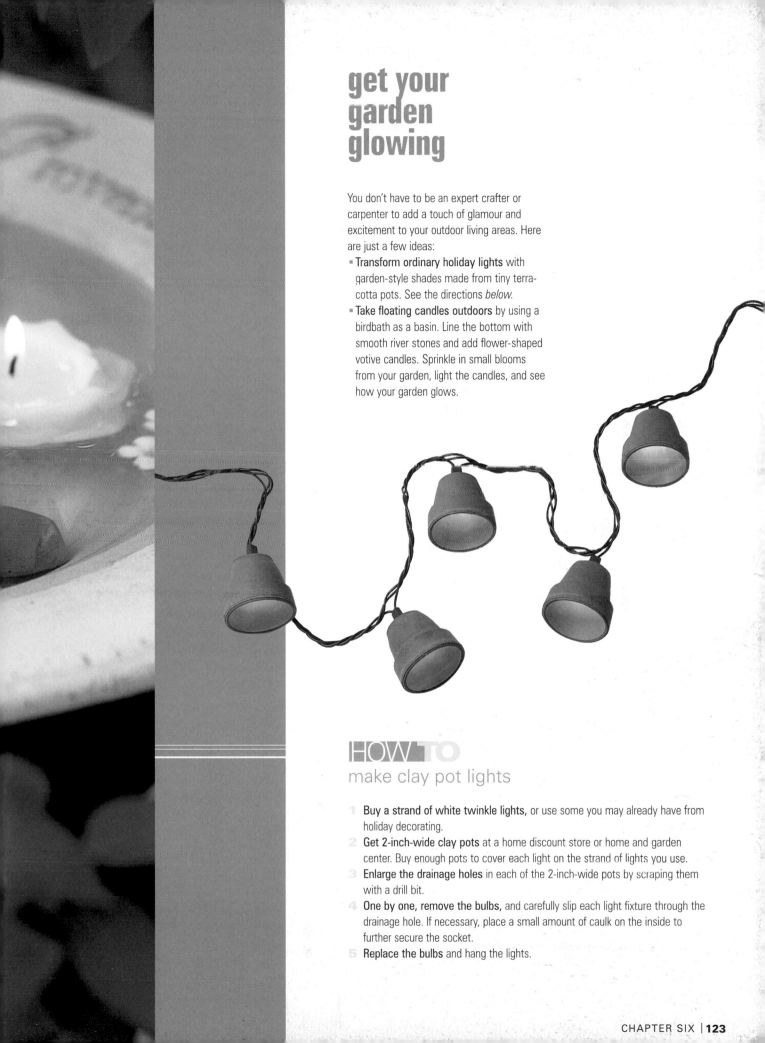

HOW TO
make clay pot lights

1. **Buy a strand of white twinkle lights,** or use some you may already have from holiday decorating.
2. **Get 2-inch-wide clay pots** at a home discount store or home and garden center. Buy enough pots to cover each light on the strand of lights you use.
3. **Enlarge the drainage holes** in each of the 2-inch-wide pots by scraping them with a drill bit.
4. **One by one, remove the bulbs,** and carefully slip each light fixture through the drainage hole. If necessary, place a small amount of caulk on the inside to further secure the socket.
5. **Replace the bulbs** and hang the lights.

display the harvest

Do you ever wish summer wouldn't end? Bring nature's mementos of fair weather indoors to enjoy when it rains or snows. Try these ideas to remind you of those sun-soaked lazy days:

- Hang a plain, Shaker-style peg rack ($10–$12 at home centers) on a porch wall, *right*, to display antique garden tools and hats (shop garage sales and junk shops for these at $2–$25 an item). Fill in with blooms from your garden or local farmer's market. Tie flowers into bunches with twine and hang upside down for colorful bouquets. To dry flowers and herbs, see the directions *below right*.
- Use orchard bounty, *below,* as an edible display. Center a substantial candle in a big glass container (a punch or salad bowl will do nicely) and fill with red or green apples.

TURN THOSE BLOOMS UPSIDE DOWN Dried flowers from your garden or the side of the road, like those *at right*, naturalize any space. Choose big blooms and many colors for variety.

SHOP FARMER'S MARKETS Check out your local farmer's markets for some of the most beautiful and low-cost items for outdoor living areas, such as the apples *below*.

HOW TO
dry bunches of flowers and herbs

1 **Cut them at the peak** of their bloom.

2 **Bind the stems together** with rubber bands.

3 **As the stems dry and shrink,** the rubber bands will keep them together. (Twine or wire will not pull in as the stems shrink, and the bundles will loosen.)

4 **Cover the rubber bands** with garden twine, leaving long loops for hanging down from the rack.

5 **Hang the bundles upside down** and allow the plants to dry naturally. This may take from several days to several weeks, depending on the moisture content of the plants and the humidity.

decorator's
tool kit glossary

So you're the budget-conscious type who likes to save decorating expenses by doing projects yourself. Any project is easier to accomplish if you have the right tools. Here are some basic supplies to keep on hand.

awl An awl, which resembles an ice pick, lets you make a starter hole or pilot hole in wood so nails and screws go in more easily.

can opener You'll need this to open a can of paint. Sometimes you can get one free with the purchase of paint. Pick up paint sticks for stirring too.

carpenter's level Don't try to "eyeball" it. Make sure your project is level by resting this tool along the surface. The bubble will be centered in the vial when the item is level. An aluminum level doubles as a straightedge for cutting.

caulk Choose a paintable acrylic or acrylic combination for indoor surfaces. It's used for sealing around bathtubs, sinks, and windows as well as for filling gaps between baseboard or crown molding and the wall.

clamps To hold objects together while you work on them or while glue sets, choose multipurpose C-clamps. Use pads when clamping wood to avoid damaging the surface.

crafts knife Check crafts stores for retractable single-blade knives and replacement blades. To get a clean cut when cutting thick materials such as mat board or foam-core board, use a new blade.

electric drill This tool is indispensable. A 1/4- or 3/8-inch drill will handle most home decorating projects.

Look for a reversible drill with variable speed control. A screwdriver bit makes quick work of installing valances, shelves, and cornices. Cordless drills are convenient if your project isn't near an electrical outlet.

fabric shears These scissors are made for (and should be reserved for) cutting fabric.

floral shears Scissors for cutting flower stems come with notched blades to provide extra leverage when cutting stems and ribbon for floral bouquets. Some shears can be taken apart for easy cleaning by hand or in the dishwasher.

glues Stock up on a variety of adhesives. For gluing fabrics, check crafts and fabric stores for washable fabric glues. For general purpose gluing of porous surfaces such as wood and paper, thick white crafts glue works well. For gluing wood to wood, use carpenter's glue. Five-minute epoxy also is recommended for adhering wood to wood, as well as for gluing nonporous surfaces such as metals, glass, porcelain, tile, and plastic.

grommet tool This tool, which is sold in fabric stores, is designed to press together the two halves of a grommet or eyelet, enclosing the fabric between them and making holes for lacing or threading.

hammer A 16-ounce claw hammer is a good all-purpose tool. The claw provides leverage for pulling nails and removing crooked ones from lumber.

handsaw Quality counts here—an inexpensive saw can chew up your wood and ruin a project. With an 8- to 10-point crosscut saw, you can cut across the grain of the wood, the most common type of sawing. (The points refer to the number of teeth per inch.) A backsaw is a type of crosscut saw with finer teeth (12 to 13 points per inch) for cutting miters. Keep saws covered with a sheath or cardboard when not in use.

hot-glue gun Every do-it-yourselfer needs at least one hot-glue gun. High-temperature glue produces the strongest bond and won't soften when exposed to sunlight or heat, but the glue can burn your skin and damage some fabrics and plastics. Low-temperature glues are less likely to burn skin or fabric, but the glue tends to soften in high-heat areas or in direct sunlight. For greatest versatility, choose a dual-temperature gun that can accept both types of glue sticks; also look for models with built-in safety stands.

paintbrushes Choose good-quality natural- or synthetic-bristle brushes for major painting projects. For small jobs or for use with acrylic crafts paints, inexpensive foam brushes work well and are disposable.

painter's tape This low-tack masking tape leaves no residue after removal. Use it to mask off areas where you don't want paint to go while you're painting an adjacent area.

pliers The two basic types you need to have on hand are slip-joint pliers and needle-nose pliers.

plumb bob Available at hardware stores, this tool is a cord with a pointed weight at one end; it's used to determine whether a vertical line is perpendicular. To use it, attach the end of the cord to the ceiling, suspending the weight just above the floor.

safety goggles Always wear goggles when scrubbing with a heavy-duty cleaner, sanding wood, using furniture stripper, or painting a ceiling.

scrapers Scrapers and putty knives come in different widths for different jobs: removing old paint, wallpaper, varnish, or glue or applying surfacing compound. Keep them clean and sharpen them often.

screwdriver For the best quality, look for cushioned, easy-grip handles and fracture-resistant bars and tips. You'll need both standard and phillips screwdrivers with tips in a variety of sizes.

sewing needles and pins Keep on hand a box of dressmaker's pins, an assortment of sewing needles, and a package of heavy-duty large-eye or tapestry needles. Quilter's pins also are good for upholstery fabrics, because they're extra long and have large plastic heads that are easy to see. T pins are heavy, T-shape pins used for temporarily securing fabric to an upholstered piece.

staple gun This is a must for stapling fabric to a chair seat or to a wood strip (for window swags). Look for one that lets you push down at the front where the staple comes out so you'll have leverage.

stud sensor If you're hanging bed canopies, window boxes, mirrors, or shelves, you'll be glad you have one of these. Electronic versions flash and beep when they locate studs, joists, and other objects; the sensor even works through extra-thick walls and floors. tack cloth Check hardware stores for this loosely woven cloth that has been treated to make it slightly sticky so it picks up sanding dust.

tape measure For sewing projects, you'll need a flexible plastic or cloth tape with a metal end. For woodworking projects, a heavy-duty retractable metal tape is helpful; the end of the tape hooks over a door frame, a window frame, or the end of a piece of wood to hold the tape in place.

window scraper With a single-edge razor holder, you can scrape paint from windows or remove sticky labels from glass.

wire cutter This clipper-like tool is handy for cutting mirror- and picture-hanging wire.

store your tools

A designated storage unit for your tools will save you both time and money—hunting down tools is a waste of time that may result in a second purchase that duplicates something you already have but can't find. If the traditional carpenter's tool chest, fishing tackle box, or antique wooden tool carrier doesn't suit your personal style, try one of these creative tool-storage ideas:

1 **Look for canvas tool bags at home centers.** Or adapt a hanging canvas clothes holder or a clear vinyl hanging shoe bag. Small- to medium-size tools slip in and out of cubbyholes or shoe slots and are easy to see. If you buy a plastic one, make sure the plastic is heavy and sturdy so sharp objects won't pierce it.

2 **Stackable plastic bins or trays** are other storage options. If you like to carry your tools with you, use a duffel bag or picnic basket. Small, often-used tools can be kept neatly in a cosmetics bag. Or check hardware stores and discount variety stores for specialty tool organizers that incorporate pockets of various sizes, stackable trays, and a step stool or bucket.

3 **Assemble a decorating closet,** a space designated to hold practical hammer-and-nail supplies as well as more creative ones, such as flower vases, candles, or party decorations. It could be a closet at the end of a hall, open shelving in the basement, an armoire with basket containers, a large trunk at the end of a bed, or a space behind a folding screen.

index